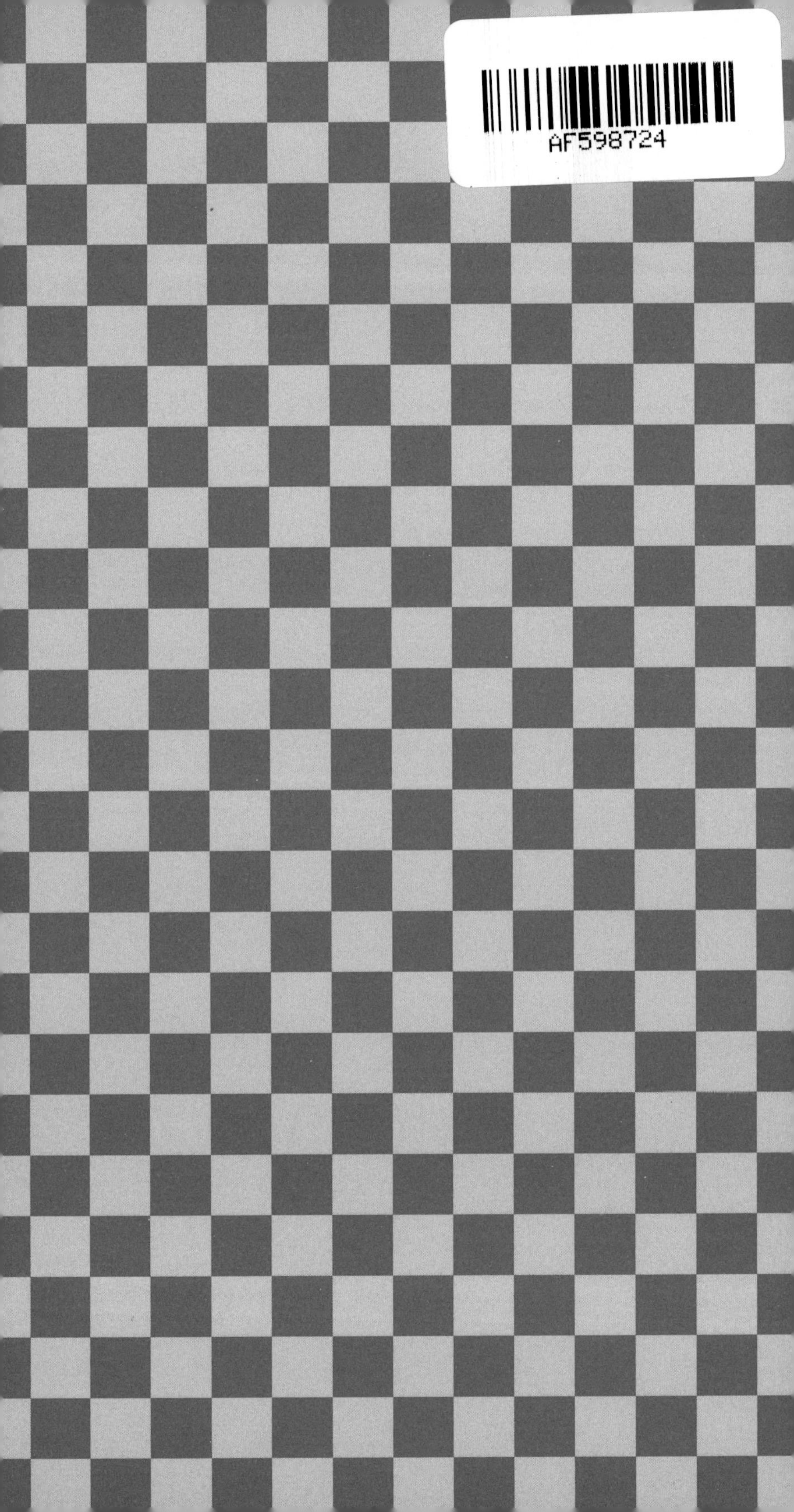

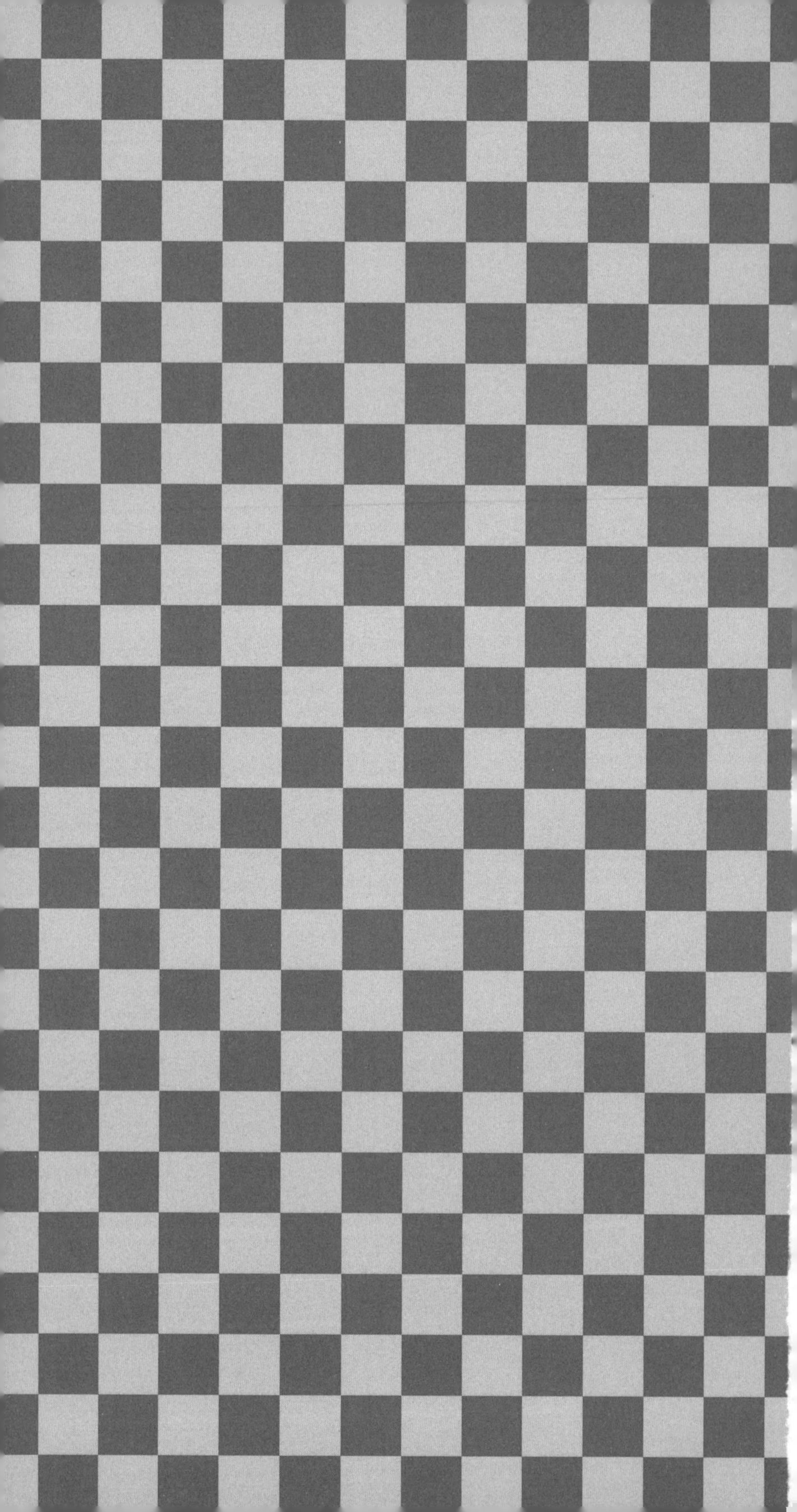

# The HOT DOG Cookbook

# The Hot Dog Cookbook

50 RECIPES FOR THE WORLD'S BEST FOOD

Farideh Sadeghin

WORKMAN PUBLISHING • NEW YORK

Workman
Workman Publishing
Hachette Book Group, Inc.
1290 Avenue of the Americas
New York, NY 10104
workman.com

Workman is an imprint of Workman Publishing, a division of Hachette Book Group, Inc. The Workman name and logo are registered trademarks of Hachette Book Group, Inc.

Design by Reagan Ruff
Illustrations by Eve Anderson



Library of Congress Cataloging-in-Publication Data

Names: Sadeghin, Farideh author
Title: The hot dog cookbook : 50 recipes for the world's best food / Farideh Sadeghin.
Description: First edition. | New York : Workman Publishing, 2026. | Includes index.
Identifiers: LCCN 2025039042 | ISBN 9781523529674 hardcover | ISBN 9781523529698 epub
Subjects: LCSH: Frankfurters | LCGFT: Cookbooks
Classification: LCC TX749.S227 2026 | DDC 641.6/6—dc23/eng/20250929
LC record available at https://lccn.loc.gov/2025039042

ISBN 978-1-5235-2967-4 (hardcover); 978-1-5235-2969-8 (ebook)

First Edition March 2026

Printed in China (APS) on responsibly sourced paper

10 9 8 7 6 5 4 3 2 1

# CONTENTS

## INTRODUCTION



## 1 AMERICAN CLASSICS



## 2 INTERNATIONAL STYLES



## 3 WILD & ORIGINAL

# INTRODUCTION

**Behold the humble hot dog.** It is arguably America's favorite food—a contentious claim to some, but perfectly reasonable and accurate to others (especially to people like you, the hot dog–loving person holding this book in their hands).

It's no surprise that this wonder food has woven itself into the American culinary tradition: Franks can be found in ballparks, convenience stores, street fairs, school cafeterias, and backyards all across the country. Hot dogs are timelessly nostalgic and endlessly adaptable. They can literally do anything.

People in other parts of the world dabble in dogs, too, and variations abound: In Latin America and Scandinavia, you'll find toppings ranging from potato chips to shrimp salad, quail eggs to crispy shallots, and remoulade to pineapple. Outside the United States, hot dogs are also more commonly included in non-bun dishes, such as Korean budae jjigae (a stew of noodles, kimchi, pork, rice cakes, and more) or Filipino spaghetti (a pasta dish made with a meat sauce sweetened with banana ketchup). Just think of the possibilities!

In this book, we're celebrating the hot dog in all its glory, including iconic American styles from New York to Alaska and all points in between, as well as international recipes from Colombia to Iceland and beyond. Plus, we're offering some original and revamped creations (Hot Dog Parmesan, anyone?).

Have I missed a variety? Undoubtedly. Got a favorite hot dog topping that you don't see here? Cool, tell me more. These recipes are based on a whole lot of research, testing, and tasting on my part. Some of the wilder ones may not exactly evoke the halcyon hot dog of your youth, but here's hoping that they bring back some pleasant and happy (or snappy?) memories.

Feel free to put your own stamp on the recipes. Use whichever hot dog brand is your favorite. (That being said, some recipes do call for specific dogs. Take the suggestion or not—it's your hot dog.) Cook it outside on the grill or inside in a pan. Steam your bun in the microwave or brown it in a toaster. It's truly *all* good—use the deliciousness and versatility of the dog for your benefit.

This book is your one-stop shop for everything hot dog. Flip through these pages to get your creative juices flowing when you're planning your next barbecue or hot dog party. (What? You've never had a hot dog party?! Get planning!) Mix and match methods, buns, dogs, and sauces. Make it meatless with a veggie dog; use a plant-based alternative for the ground beef in the chili sauce recipes. Top your dog with something you never even dreamed of before. Have fun and get messy. Forget oysters—the world is your hot dog.

## A Brief History of Hot Dogs (and Sausages)

To truly know the hot dog, we must first understand the sausage. You see, hot dogs are a proud member of the weird and wonderful family of sausages. And while all hot dogs are sausages, not all sausages are hot dogs. (Make sense yet? Stay with us.)

The key differences are in their ingredients and how they're served. Sausages tend to contain more spices, while a hot dog is usually milder. The meat in hot dogs is more finely ground than that of most sausages, and hot dogs are almost always precooked, while sausages typically come fresh. And let's be honest: A hot dog really becomes a hot dog when it's nestled in a bun.

### Tubular Meats Through the Ages

Hot dog history is murky and complicated, but there are some key milestones:

- Archaeological evidence suggests that sausages appeared some 20,000 years ago, during the Upper Paleolithic Period; most likely they were meats cooked in skins over open fire.
- One of the earliest known literary references to sausage is found in Homer's *Odyssey*, some 3,000 years ago: "As when a man besides a great fire has filled a sausage with fat and blood and turns it this way and that and is very eager to get it quickly roasted . . ." (Relatable.)
- A cook for the Roman emperor Nero named Gaius is credited with discovering sausage casing in 64 CE. He realized that a pig had been roasted without first being gutted, and when he slit

open its belly, the intestines spilled out hollow (due to starvation) and puffed (due to the heat of the oven). Bada bing, bada boom, sausage casings.

- Sausages were an important food in the Middle Ages. Because they were smoked or cured in salt it meant people could eat meat throughout the long, cold winters.
- When Europeans came to North America, they brought with them their culinary traditions, among them the art of sausage making. There are several American sausage varieties (see a brief tutorial on page 70), many of which can be used in place of hot dogs in the recipes in this book. The first cookbook published in the American colonies in 1730, *The Compleat Housewife* by Eliza Smith, also happens to be the first cookbook to contain a recipe for fresh pork sausage.
- Prior to the American Civil War, sausages were made by hand, and even then people were dubious about what butchers were stuffing into the casings. Numerous recipes from sausage-makers' cookbooks called for meat trimmings, offal, and scraps.
- Around 1868, sausage production changed forever with the introduction of the first steam-powered meat chopper, allowing 100 pounds of meat to be chopped in only 30 minutes.
- Sometime in the 1880s, Frankfurt- and Vienna-style sausages (the closest relatives of modern hot dogs) are placed *inside* buns. It's a match made in heaven.
- In the watershed year of 1893, frankfurters became a favorite food at the Chicago World's Fair, where beloved Chi-Town hot dog brand Vienna Beef made its debut. Hot dogs also became standard fare at baseball stadiums that year.
- German immigrants had been pushing hot dog carts around since the 1860s, usually offering mustard and/or relish as toppings. But one man is generally credited with popularizing the American hot dog: Nathan Handwerker, a Jewish immigrant from Poland. After working at a famous Coney Island hot dog stand owned by Charles Feltman, Handwerker opened his own stand in 1916 that would evolve into the iconic Nathan's Famous.
- In 1939, President Franklin D. Roosevelt served hot dogs to Queen Elizabeth and King George VI of England. The king loved them so much he reportedly asked for seconds. (In a major breach of hot dog etiquette, the queen used a knife and fork—oh, the horror!)
- After becoming an American staple during the Great Depression, hot dogs found creative regional flair and eventually went global. The world is now a better place.

## Anatomy of a Hot Dog

Many people continue to question what's inside of hot dogs and how they're made, but production has come a long way, and you can find really great artisanal hot dogs on the market (see some suggestions in Resources, page 130).

Nowadays, hot dogs are made by grinding and mixing meat trimmings (muscle meat, no longer scraps) with spices. Different brands use different spice blends, but garlic, paprika, mace, allspice, coriander, nutmeg, salt, pepper, and ground mustard are common ingredients, as well as curing agents like sodium nitrite (which affect flavor and color). Once properly ground and blended into an emulsion, the mixture is fed into tubes that are connected to casings (either natural or synthetic). They're then cut into hot dog lengths—typically about 6 inches—to be cooked and smoked.

### *Skinless or natural-casing?*

Skinless hot dogs don't grill as well as those with skins; after charring and plumping on the grates, they tend to shrivel when removed from direct heat. The exterior can get dry and leather-like, although the interior remains fairly moist. Making a couple of slashes in a skinless dog helps prevent this by allowing it to heat through more quickly, but they're still not ideal. Plus, slashing hot dogs releases some of their juices, so they tend to dry out a bit.

Hot dogs with natural casings (i.e., sheep or pig intestines) have more snap when you bite into them. They also hold up better on the grill. I don't recommend slashing these dogs, unless you want all those good juices to bubble out and spill over onto the grill grates.

### *Cured or uncured?*

Here's another main difference you'll often see on hot dog packages. Cured hot dogs are typically preserved with either sodium nitrate or sodium nitrite and have a bright pink color, longer shelf life, and that classic "cured meat" flavor. Uncured hot dogs are preserved using naturally occurring nitrates found in ingredients like celery powder, celery juice, or beet juice.

## Cooking Methods

The recipes in this book call for several ways of cooking hot dogs. Grilling a dog in summer might be your favorite, but sometimes it's cold and rainy, so steaming, baking, or microwaving might end up being the method you have to roll with. Listed below are all the ways you can cook your hot dog.

- **Steam:** Place a steamer basket in a large saucepan and add about an inch of water. Cover and bring to a simmer over medium heat. Add the hot dogs to the steamer basket and cover the pan. Steam until the hot dogs are plump and warmed through, 4 to 6 minutes. Carefully remove the hot dogs using tongs, taking care not to burn yourself.
- **Boil:** Bring a large saucepan of water to a boil. Reduce the heat to maintain a low simmer. Add the hot dogs and cook until heated through, 4 to 5 minutes (don't boil them much longer; overcooking can result in wrinkly or burst wieners). Alternatively, poach them in a couple bottles of beer (enough to cover the hot dogs) for the same amount of time for an even more flavorful dog. Clean and crisp lagers work well with your classic dog, while pilsners work nicely with German-style dogs and toasty, malty amber ales are great with spicy hot dogs. (Avoid sour or overly bitter beers.)
- **Microwave:** Place the hot dogs on a plate and cook on high for 45 seconds to 1 minute, or until the center of the hot dog is warm to the touch.
- **Grill:** Light a grill. Add the hot dogs and cook, turning as needed, until golden and plump, 3 to 4 minutes.

- **Bake:** Heat the oven to 400°F. Place the hot dogs on a sheet pan and cook until plumped and beginning to brown, 12 to 15 minutes.
- **Air-fry:** Heat the air fryer to 400°F. Add the hot dogs and cook for 3 to 4 minutes until golden and warmed through.
- **Deep-fry:** Heat 2 inches of vegetable oil in a large, heavy saucepan or deep fryer until a thermometer reads 350°F. Add the hot dogs and cook until golden, 2 to 3 minutes. Then, using a slotted spoon or metal tongs, remove the hot dogs and transfer to a paper towel–lined plate before adding it to the prepared bun. Be sure not to overcrowd the fryer.
- **Over a campfire:** Thread a hot dog onto a metal skewer. Carefully hold the hot dog over the fire and cook, rotating every 30 seconds or so, until lightly golden and plump, 2 to 3 minutes. Make sure it doesn't catch on fire!
- **Pan-fry:** Heat 2 tablespoons of oil in a large skillet over medium-high heat. Add the hot dogs and cook, turning as needed, until golden and plump, 2 to 3 minutes.
- **Hydrotoast:** Pour enough water in a medium saucepan to reach about ¼-inch depth and bring to a boil over high. Reduce the heat to maintain a simmer and add the hot dogs. Cook, uncovered, until the water has reduced, 5 to 7 minutes. Allow the hot dogs to continue cooking, turning as needed, until golden all over, 4 to 5 minutes longer.
- **Broil:** Heat the broiler to high. Place the hot dogs on a sheet pan and cook, rotating the pan halfway through, until plumped and beginning to brown, 4 to 5 minutes.

## Other cooking tips:

- No need to poke or slit the hot dog to check for doneness; hot dogs are precooked, and doing either will release their precious juices. Don't you want your hot dog to stay juicy?!
- Make sure hot dogs are defrosted before cooking them, no matter the method.
- Don't place hot dogs over direct flame or high heat. Indirect grilling is best; you'll still get color on the dog, and it will be heated through. Cooking over high heat or flame will result in bursting (although you may want to achieve those exact results when making New Jersey rippers—see page 48).

## Buns

What makes a good bun? The number and type of toppings that you're adding to your hot dog will help determine the best bun size and heating method. Steaming will result in a soft, pillowy roll, while toasting or grilling will add great flavor and enough heft to stand up to the weight of more toppings and sauces. (Pro tip: Prepare the buns before you start cooking the hot dogs. That ensures there's no need for a plate—the bun is in hand and ready for the cooked dog.)

- **Steam:** To steam in a microwave, individually wrap each bun in a damp paper towel and cook on high for about 20 seconds. To steam on the stovetop, place a steamer basket in a large saucepan and add about an inch of water. Cover and bring to a simmer over medium heat. Add the buns to the steamer basket and cover the pan. Steam for 2 minutes, then carefully remove using tongs, taking care not to burn yourself on the steam.
- **Grill:** Light a grill. For traditional hot dog buns, you don't need to oil or butter the inside. For hardier options like pizza bread or a baguette, oil the insides lightly. Grill the bun or bread cut side down until golden, 1 to 2 minutes.
- **Pan-fry:** Brush the inside of the bun with oil. Add the bun to a nonstick pan or cast-iron skillet, cut side down over medium-high, and cook until golden, about 2 minutes.

# Other Basics

## How to Store Hot Dogs After Opening

- Hot dogs will last in the refrigerator, unopened, for up to 2 weeks.
- Once opened, store in an airtight container or bag in the refrigerator for up to 1 week.
- Alternatively, freeze uncooked hot dogs in an airtight container for up to 2 months.

## Why are buns sold in packages of 8, and hot dogs in packages of 10?

Here's a fun fact: According to the National Hot Dog and Sausage Council, buns most often come eight to the pack because the buns are baked in clusters of four. Okay, so what do these configurations mean for you, humble buyer of hot dog buns? To break even and have no waste, you'd need to buy five bags of buns to accommodate four packs of hot dogs. (That's a lotta dogs.)

That being said, after shopping for a whole lotta hot dogs for this cookbook, I've found many varieties in supermarkets that come in packs of eight. There are also *lots* of recipes in this book that require no bun at all, so don't stress about this ever-evolving little hot dog curiosity.

## Fun Ways to Cut a Hot Dog

- **Octopus (aka "octodog"):** Cut the hot dog in half crosswise. The top half will be the "head," and the bottom will be the "tentacles." Leaving about 1½ inches uncut for the head and starting at one end, make lengthwise cuts up the hot dog to create tentacles by first cutting the hot dog in half, then in quarters, and finally in eighths (this is an octopus, after all, so you're going to want eight tentacles). You're basically cutting strips upward from the bottom. To cook, either boil, microwave, pan-fry, or air-fry.

- **Crosshatched:** Lay the hot dog flat on a cutting board. Make diagonal cuts across the surface of the hot dog, about ⅛ to ¼ inch deep, spaced ½ inch apart. Don't cut too deep—you want to score the hot dog, not slice through it. Rotate the hot dog 90 degrees and repeat diagonal cuts in the opposite direction, creating a diamond (crosshatch) pattern. The ideal way to cook these bad boys is by grilling, pan-frying, or in an air fryer. Not only does it look cute, but the hot dog will cook more evenly and absorb toppings or sauces better.
- **Butterflied:** Slice the hot dog lengthwise about 80 percent of the way through—you want the two halves to stay connected like a hinge. It cooks faster, gets more crispy edges, and lays flat in a bun. It's best cooked by grilling, pan-frying, or air-frying.

- **Fish-scaled:** Lay the hot dog flat on a cutting board. Start near one end and, using your knife, make a series of shallow crescent-shaped cuts like little "smiles" going across the surface of the hot dog. The cuts should be evenly spaced and about ¼ inch deep. For the next row, offset the crescents so they sit between the ones above, like laying shingles on a house. Continue this staggered crescent pattern down the length of the frank. Cook it by either grilling, pan-searing, air-frying, or baking. The scale pattern will really pop once it's cooked.
- **Spiralized:** Insert a skewer through the length of the hot dog, then, holding a paring knife at a 45-degree angle, cut the meat in a spiral by twirling the hot dog as you cut down the length. Remove the skewer and grill or pan-fry, turning as needed, until golden, about 3 minutes.

## Best Sides to Serve with Hot Dogs

- Fries
- Potato chips
- Potato salad
- Macaroni salad
- Pasta salad
- Grilled corn
- Baked beans
- Coleslaw
- Onion rings
- Even more hot dogs

## *Hot Dog Etiquette*

### DO

- Dress the dog, not the bun.
- Add condiments in this order: wet (mustard, ketchup, mayo, chili), chunky (onion, relish, sauerkraut), shredded cheese, crispy stuff (fries), spices.

### DON'T

- Eat a hot dog with a fork and knife. Hands only!
- Leave the bun on your plate, like you would pizza crust. Eat it all or eat nothing (or feed extra bun to the dog).
- Use cloth napkins . . . paper only, please!

## A Not-at-All Complete List of Hot Dog Toppings

### *(Because Literally Everything Can Go on a Dog)*

- Mustard (in all its varieties)
- Ketchup
- Sauerkraut
- Relish
- Mayonnaise
- Salsa rosada (a mixture of ketchup and mayo)
- Remoulade
- Crispy shallots
- Chutney
- Pickled or fresh jalapeños
- Hot dog chili sauce
- Cheese
- Cream cheese
- Diced raw or grilled onions (white, yellow, red, spring)
- Store-bought crispy fried onions
- Fries
- Potato chips/sticks
- Pineapple
- Bacon
- Eggs
- Tomatoes
- Corn
- Peas
- Avocados
- Guacamole
- Sport peppers
- Celery salt
- Pickles
- Sour cream
- Yes, literally everything!

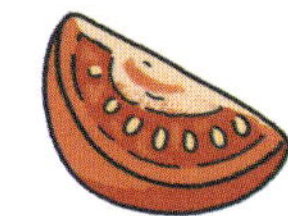

1
American Classics

# CONEY DOGS

Brooklyn's Coney Island is arguably the birthplace of American hot dogs, but this dog topped with meat sauce, yellow mustard, and onions has Midwestern roots. Most likely the Coney dog arrived by way of Greek immigrants in Michigan. This classic Detroit-based sauce is looser than versions found in Flint or Jackson, which are referred to as "dry" (not in a bad way) and typically include beef heart for an extra bang of meaty flavor.

**MAKES 8**

**For the coney sauce**

2 tablespoons vegetable oil

1 medium yellow onion, diced

1 pound (454 grams) ground beef

2 tablespoons chili powder

1 tablespoon ground cumin

½ teaspoon celery salt

½ teaspoon garlic powder

8 ounces (225 grams) tomato sauce

2 tablespoons Worcestershire sauce

1 tablespoon yellow mustard

Kosher salt and freshly ground black pepper to taste

**For the hot dogs**

8 hot dogs

8 hot dog buns

1 large yellow onion, finely diced

Yellow mustard

### The United States of Coney

There are Coney dog variations sprinkled throughout the United States: Michigan Red Hots can be found in Plattsburgh, New York, and in Ohio, where Cincinnati-style Coneys come loaded with shredded Cheddar cheese. If you're into cute little hot dogs, check out the 3-inch minis in Troy, New York (topped with a meat sauce known as "Zippy Sauce") at the well-known local hot doggery Famous Lunch.

**1. Make the sauce:** Heat the oil in a medium saucepan over medium-high heat. Add the onion and cook until soft, about 3 minutes. Add the beef and cook, stirring and breaking it up with a wooden spoon, until browned, about 5 minutes more.

**2.** Add the chili powder, cumin, celery salt, and garlic powder and cook for 2 minutes, then stir in the tomato sauce, Worcestershire sauce, mustard, and 2 cups (500 ml) of water. Lower the heat to maintain a simmer and cook until thick, about 1 hour. Season with salt and pepper and keep warm.

**3. Make the hot dogs:** Cook the hot dogs on a flattop grill or in a pan (see pages 5 and 6). Steam the buns (see page 7).

**4.** To assemble, place each hot dog in a bun and top each with some of the sauce. Sprinkle with finely diced onions, then drizzle with mustard and serve.

# SONORAN DOGS

Popular throughout Arizona, especially in Tucson, this bacon-wrapped, topping-heavy hot dog originated in the 1970s in Hermosillo, the capital of the Mexican state of Sonora. Its special bolillo-style roll is incredibly soft and usually steamed, and it comes with a couple of charred chiles güeros on the side. I recommend regular (not thick-cut) bacon for this recipe because it won't require toothpicks to secure it to the hot dog.

**MAKES 8**

**For the jalapeño sauce**

4 jalapeños (about 8 ounces/225 grams), stemmed and seeded (but don't be afraid to leave in some seeds for extra heat!)

1 garlic clove, peeled

½ medium yellow onion, peeled

2 tablespoons vegetable oil

Kosher salt and freshly ground black pepper to taste

**For the hot dogs**

8 jumbo hot dogs

8 slices bacon

1 can (15.5 ounces/439 grams) pinto beans, rinsed and drained

2 tablespoons vegetable oil

2 medium white onions, thinly sliced

8 bolillo-style rolls

2 medium tomatoes, diced

2 avocados, halved, peeled, pitted, and diced

Mayonnaise

Mustard

**1. Make the jalapeño sauce:** Place the jalapeños, garlic, and onion in a small saucepan and add water to cover. Bring to a boil, then reduce the heat to low. Simmer until the jalapeños are soft, about 15 minutes. Drain, discarding the cooking liquid. Allow the vegetables to cool slightly, then transfer to a blender and puree until smooth. With the motor running, stream in the oil, blending until creamy. Season with salt.

**2. Make the hot dogs:** Wrap each hot dog in a slice of bacon and set aside.

**3.** Wipe the saucepan clean, then add the beans and place over medium heat. Cook until warmed through, 3 to 5 minutes. Season with salt and pepper and keep warm.

*(continues)*

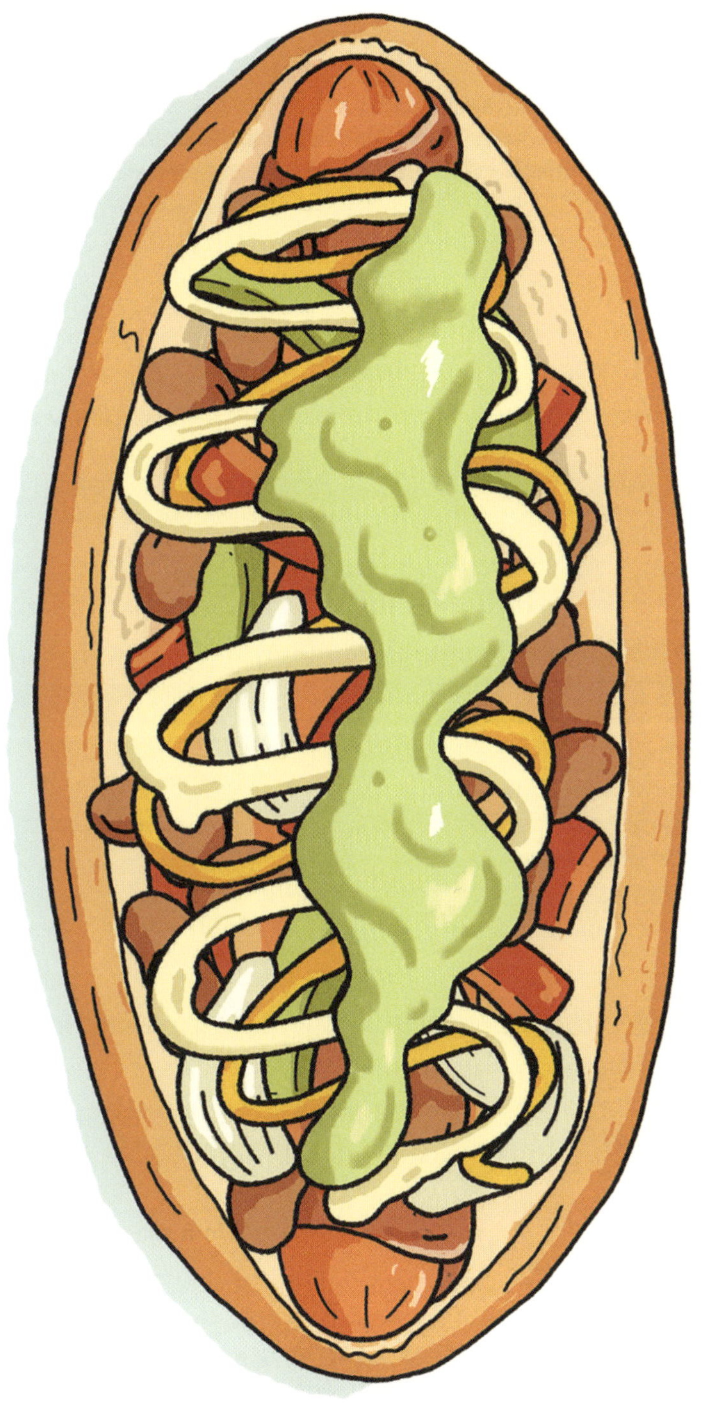

**4.** Heat the oil in a large skillet over medium-high. Add the onions and cook, stirring, until golden, 7 to 8 minutes. Season with salt, then remove from the skillet and set aside until ready to use.

**5.** Reduce the heat to medium and add the hot dogs to the skillet. Cook, rotating as needed, until the bacon is crisp, about 7 minutes.

**6.** Steam the hot dog rolls (see page 7).

**7.** To assemble, place a hot dog in each of the steamed buns, then top with the onions, beans, tomatoes, and avocado. Drizzle on the jalapeño sauce, mayonnaise, and mustard and serve.

***A Note on the Bun*** • Not quite a bolillo roll and *definitely* not your average hot dog bun, this slightly sweet bread (sometimes called a "doggo bun") is in a league all its own. Steamed until incredibly soft, it can still hold all the extras and toppings thrown onto it without falling apart. Another roll or bun would work in a pinch, but it's worth seeking out the real deal from a local Mexican bakery or market.

# CHICAGO DOGS

The Windy City's love for hot dogs runs deep, and its namesake Chicago dog is inarguably the town's most iconic creation. Chicagoans are sticklers for what goes on a proper Chicago dog (and in what order toppings are applied), loading it with a variety of veggies until it's "dragged it through the garden." But no matter what you do, remember these words: Do. Not. Add. Ketchup.

**MAKES 8**

8 all-beef hot dogs

8 poppy seed hot dog buns

Yellow mustard

2 tomatoes, cut into rounds, then halved

8 dill pickle spears

Chopped onion

Chicago-style relish (or sweet pickle relish)

16 sport peppers (purchasable in some regions and online)

Celery salt

**1.** Cook the hot dogs using whatever method you choose—steamed, boiled, or grilled (see pages 5–6)—although steaming or boiling is the most traditional method. Steam the buns (see page 7).

**2.** To assemble, place the hot dogs in the buns and drizzle with mustard. Nestle a couple of tomato slices on one side of the hot dog and a pickle spear on the other side. Top each hot dog with the onion and relish, plus two of the sport peppers. Sprinkle with the celery salt and serve.

# NEW YORK SYSTEM HOT WIENERS

Sometimes also called gaggers, and traditionally made with a combination of veal, beef, and pork, these curiously named hot dogs are a Rhode Island staple. The meat sauce evolved from Providence's Greek immigrant population, and it contains a variety of warming spices that differentiate it from other chili recipes.

**MAKES 8**

**For the chili sauce**

2 tablespoons vegetable oil

1 medium yellow onion, minced

1 pound (454 grams) ground beef

2 tablespoons Worcestershire sauce

1 tablespoon chili powder

1 tablespoon ground cumin

1 tablespoon sweet paprika

1 teaspoon ground cinnamon

1 teaspoon dry mustard

¾ teaspoon ground allspice

Kosher salt and freshly ground black pepper to taste

**For the hot dogs**

8 hot dogs

8 hot dog buns

Yellow mustard

1 medium white onion, minced

Celery salt

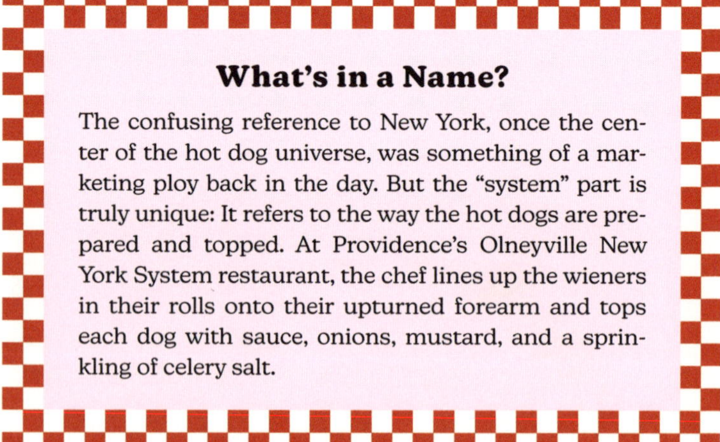

### What's in a Name?

The confusing reference to New York, once the center of the hot dog universe, was something of a marketing ploy back in the day. But the "system" part is truly unique: It refers to the way the hot dogs are prepared and topped. At Providence's Olneyville New York System restaurant, the chef lines up the wieners in their rolls onto their upturned forearm and tops each dog with sauce, onions, mustard, and a sprinkling of celery salt.

*(continues)*

**1. Make the chili sauce:** Heat the oil in a medium saucepan over medium-high heat. Add the onion and cook until soft, 3 to 4 minutes. Add the beef and cook, stirring and breaking it up with a wooden spoon, until browned, about 5 minutes. Add the Worcestershire sauce, chili powder, cumin, paprika, cinnamon, dry mustard, allspice, and 2 cups (500 ml) of water, stirring to combine. Bring to a simmer, then reduce the heat to medium-low and cook until thick, about 45 minutes. Season with salt and pepper and keep warm.

**2. Make the hot dogs:** Cook the hot dogs in a skillet (see page 6). Steam the buns (see page 7).

**3.** To assemble, place the hot dogs in the buns and drizzle with the mustard. Top each with some of the chili sauce and the onion, then sprinkle with celery salt and serve.

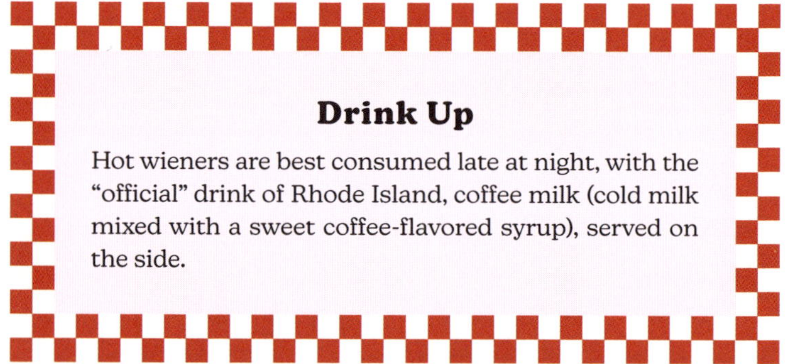

## Drink Up

Hot wieners are best consumed late at night, with the "official" drink of Rhode Island, coffee milk (cold milk mixed with a sweet coffee-flavored syrup), served on the side.

# A Brief History of KETCHUP

A whopping 97 percent of Americans keep a bottle of ketchup hiding somewhere in their refrigerator or pantry. And an estimated 61 percent slather it on their hot dog, making it second only to mustard as the most popular condiment. So how did we get here?

Eighteenth-century cookbooks offered "catsup" recipes that used all manner of ingredients, such as oysters, mushrooms, lemons, fruits, and spices. These were boiled down into pastes or fermented with salt. The resulting product was something that had a long shelf life and could be taken on extended voyages. Many Europeans initially considered tomatoes poisonous due to their acidity, but by the early nineteenth century tomatoes made their way into ketchup.

Jonas Yerkes is credited with selling the first nationally distributed ketchup, but it wasn't until 1876 that Henry J. Heinz began producing his company's signature blend of tomatoes, vinegar, brown sugar, salt, and spices sold in clear glass jars. Before that, ketchup was sold in brown bottles (a tactic used to hide the poor quality).

Heinz also popularized spelling the sauce's name as "ketchup." From there, other companies began producing and selling ketchup varieties using the once-thought-to-be-poisonous tomato, and, well, the rest is history. (To this day, some mustard-lovers consider ketchup on a hot dog to be highly poisonous.)

# DENVER DOGS

Colorado is rightfully known for its green chiles. Though often mistaken for New Mexican Hatch chiles, Colorado pueblo chiles have thicker skins, thought to be a result of the higher altitude at which they're grown. Either way, visit the Centennial State and you'll probably find green chile on the menu at many restaurants—and especially on a hot dog. Sour cream helps tame the heat, while diced red onion and sliced jalapeños add a fresh punch.

**MAKES 8**

**For the green chile sauce**

12 ounces (340 grams) boneless pork butt, cut into ½-inch pieces

2 teaspoons all-purpose flour

1 teaspoon kosher salt, plus more to taste

2 tablespoons vegetable oil

1 medium yellow onion, finely chopped

½ teaspoon ground cumin

2 garlic cloves, minced

2 cups (500 ml) chicken stock

4 cans (4 ounces/113 grams) diced green chiles

**For the hot dogs**

8 hot dogs

8 hot dog buns

Sour cream

2 jalapeños, thinly sliced

1 small red onion, finely chopped

**1. Make the green chile sauce:** In a medium bowl, toss the pork with the flour and 1 teaspoon of the salt. Heat the oil in a medium saucepan over medium-high heat. Working in batches, cook the pork, turning occasionally, until golden, 4 to 5 minutes per batch. Transfer the pork to a bowl.

**2.** Add the onion to the pan and cook, stirring, until lightly golden, about 3 minutes, then stir in the cumin and garlic and cook until fragrant, about 1 minute more. Add the stock and stir, scraping up the browned bits from the bottom of the pan, then return the pork to the saucepan along with the green chiles. Bring to a simmer over medium-low heat and cook until the pork is very tender and the sauce is thick, about 1 hour.

**3. Make the hot dogs:** Grill the hot dogs (see page 5). Grill the buns (see page 7).

**4.** To assemble, place the hot dogs in the buns and top each with some green chile sauce. Add a dollop of sour cream, then sprinkle with jalapeños and onion and serve.

# HALF-SMOKES

Washington, DC's signature half-smoke is a bit smoky, a bit spicy, and entirely delicious. It remains unclear who exactly invented the half-smoke or what the "half" even refers to; some say it's because the meat is half pork and half beef, or because it's kind of like a hot dog/sausage hybrid (it's certainly dog enough for this book). No matter—these dogs rule the town, and by far the most well-known spot is Ben's Chili Bowl on U Street. Open since 1958, their iconic dog is dished out on a steamed bun and topped "all the way" with chili sauce, diced onions, and yellow mustard.

**MAKES 8**

### For the chili sauce

2 tablespoons vegetable oil

1 medium yellow onion, diced

1 medium green bell pepper, stemmed, seeded, and diced

3 tablespoons chili powder

2 teaspoons dehydrated onion

1 teaspoon cayenne

1 teaspoon dry mustard

1 teaspoon garlic powder

1 teaspoon ground cumin

1 teaspoon smoked paprika

1 pound (454 grams) ground beef

2 garlic cloves, minced

¼ cup (80 grams) tomato paste

2 medium tomatoes, grated, skin discarded

Kosher salt and freshly ground black pepper to taste

### For the sausages

8 regular half-smoke sausages

8 split-top hot dog buns

Yellow mustard

Diced raw white onions

**1. Make the chili sauce:** Heat the oil in a medium saucepan over medium-high. Add the diced onion and cook until soft, about 3 minutes, then stir in the diced bell pepper. Cook until soft, about 3 minutes more, then add the chili powder, dehydrated onion, cayenne, dry mustard, garlic powder, cumin, and paprika. Cook for 2 minutes, then stir in the ground beef. Cook, stirring, until the beef is cooked through, about 4 minutes. Stir in the garlic and cook until fragrant, about 2 minutes. Add the tomato paste and cook for 2 minutes, then stir in the grated tomatoes. Cook for 2 to 3 minutes until the tomatoes have softened slightly, then stir in 3 cups (750 ml) of water. Bring to a simmer over medium-low heat and cook until thick, about 1 hour. Season to taste with salt and pepper, then use a blender (an immersion blender is easiest) to blend the sauce slightly.

**2. Make the sausages:** Grill the sausages (see page 5). Steam the buns (see page 7).

**3.** To assemble, place the sausages in the buns and spread some mustard over the top, then sprinkle with the onions. Spoon some chili sauce on each and enjoy.

***Pro Tip*** • You can order Ben's half-smokes (and their chili sauce) online, but kielbasa or andouille sausages are good alternatives.

# IDAHO DOGS

It's unclear whether you can find this hot dog anywhere *in* the Potato State, but spuds are certainly the star of the show here. (Plus, for all you gluten-free folks out there, using a baked potato as a bun is ideal.) Be sure to take care when fluffing the potato's insides, as you want to leave it as structurally intact as possible while also making sure it's soft enough for eating. Got other toppings you enjoy on a baked potato? Throw 'em on!

**MAKES 8**

8 russet potatoes, scrubbed clean

Olive oil for drizzling

Kosher salt and freshly ground black pepper to taste

8 ounces (225 grams) bacon, diced

8 hot dogs

8 tablespoons (113 grams) unsalted butter

4 ounces (125 grams) finely shredded Cheddar cheese

8 ounces (225 grams) sour cream

3 scallions, thinly sliced

**1.** Heat the oven to 425°F. Place the potatoes on individual pieces of aluminum foil and drizzle each with olive oil, then season all over with salt. Wrap in the foil, then place the potatoes on a sheet pan. Bake until tender, about 1 hour. Set aside until cool enough to handle, 5 to 10 minutes.

**2.** While the potatoes are baking, place the bacon in a large skillet and cook over medium heat, stirring occasionally, until crisp, about 9 minutes. Using a slotted spoon, transfer the bacon to a paper towel–lined plate.

**3.** Cook the hot dogs by steaming them (see page 5), although, since you have your oven on, you could pop them in there, too (see page 5). Pro tip: Cook the hot dogs in a skillet (see pan-fry method on page 6) using some of the bacon fat!

**4.** Working with one potato at a time, cut a wedge from the center of the potato, about ¾ inch wide and 1 inch deep (big enough to nestle your hot dog into it). Remove the skin from the wedge and discard the skin.

*(continues)*

**5.** Transfer the potato wedge to a bowl and add 4 tablespoons of the butter. Cut and peel wedges from the remaining potatoes and add to the bowl with the butter. Using a fork, mash the potato wedges with the butter and season with salt and pepper. Keep warm.

**6.** Still working with one potato at a time and using the tines of a fork, lightly mash the inside of the potato, taking care not to scrape into the skin. Leave a bit of a shell to hold the potato in shape.

**7.** Add ½ tablespoon of butter to each potato "bun" and season with salt. Allow the butter to melt, then mix with the fork.

**8.** To assemble, top each potato with a hot dog, then top each dog with some of the potato mixture and sprinkle with the cheese. Place a dollop of sour cream on top, then sprinkle with the bacon and scallions and serve.

# POLISH BOYS

Cleveland's signature hot dog is often referred to as a sandwich, but we'll get to that thorny subject later (see page 102) and just enjoy the fact that we've got ourselves a hot dog with fries piled on top. (Yes, this is something to celebrate.) Typically made with kielbasa, the Polish boy also features a heap of coleslaw (either vinegar-based or mayo—dealer's choice) and barbecue sauce. The result? It's kind of like all your favorite barbecue dishes and sides piled into a bun.

**MAKES 8**

**For the slaw**

12 ounces (340 grams) green cabbage, shredded

¼ cup (60 grams) mayonnaise

2 tablespoons minced yellow onion

2 tablespoons white vinegar

2 teaspoons yellow mustard

¼ teaspoon celery seeds

Kosher salt and freshly ground black pepper to taste

**For the sausages**

1 bag (1 pound 10 ounces/ 737 grams) frozen classic French fries

8 kielbasa sausage links, about 3 ounces each

8 hot dog buns

Barbecue sauce (page 50, or use store-bought)

**1. Make the slaw:** In a large bowl, mix together the cabbage, mayonnaise, onion, vinegar, mustard, and celery seeds. Season with salt and pepper. Cover and chill until ready to serve.

**2.** Cook the fries according to the package instructions.

**3. Make the sausages:** Grill the kielbasa (see page 5). Toast or steam the buns (see page 7).

**4.** To assemble, place a kielbasa in each bun. Top each with some of the fries, coleslaw, and a drizzle of barbecue sauce and serve.

# CLASSIC CORN DOGS

Although beloved at state fairs throughout the United States and beyond, the corn dog was born in the small town of Rockaway Beach on the Oregon Coast. (This original version, known affectionately as a pronto pup, features a slightly sweeter pancake-like batter rather than a classic corn dog's cornbread-like batter.) No matter what you call it, we love a hot dog on a stick, and this recipe hits the spot.

**MAKES 8**

- 8 bamboo skewers
- 8 hot dogs
- 1 tablespoon vegetable oil, plus more for frying
- 1½ cups (250 grams) fine yellow cornmeal
- 1¼ cups (175 grams) all-purpose flour
- ¼ cup (60 grams) granulated sugar
- 1 tablespoon baking powder
- 1 teaspoon kosher salt
- 1¾ cups (430 ml) buttermilk
- 1 large egg
- Ketchup
- Mustard

**1.** Trim your skewers to around 7 or 8 inches, if necessary, so that they can fit in the fryer. Insert the skewers into the hot dogs, taking care not to pierce through the opposite ends and leaving enough room for you to hold the end of the skewer. Dry the dogs with a clean paper towel and set aside until ready to use.

**2.** Meanwhile, heat 3 inches of oil in a large, heavy saucepan until a deep-fry thermometer reads 350°F.

**3.** In a large bowl, stir together the cornmeal, flour, sugar, baking powder, and salt. In a separate large bowl, whisk together the buttermilk, the 1 tablespoon of oil, and the egg. Whisk the wet ingredients into the cornmeal mixture until smooth. Transfer some of the batter into a pint glass or jar, leaving about 1 inch at the top. (You'll refill the glass with more batter as you coat more hot dogs.)

**4.** Working with one hot dog at a time, hold on to the wooden skewer and dip the hot dog into the batter in the pint glass, coating the dog. Carefully holding the end of the skewer, dip the coated hot dog into the hot oil, turning it to help set the batter, then drop it into the oil. Fry the corn dog, using tongs to rotate it, until the batter has set and is golden, about 4 minutes. Transfer to a paper towel–lined plate and repeat coating and frying the remaining hot dogs.

**5.** Serve with ketchup and mustard.

## Korean Corn Dogs

Corn dogs are incredibly popular in South Korea, where they also fill the batter with ingredients like cheese, rice cakes, or fish cakes. Ramen and fries are sometimes included in the batter, which is usually made with rice flour rather than corn flour.

# A Brief History of MUSTARD

The story of mustard goes *waaay* back to as far as 3000 BCE. Sumerian texts refer to the use of mustard seeds as a spice, and ancient Greeks and Romans extolled mustard for its health benefits. The Greek physician Hippocrates, for instance, prescribed mustard packs to relieve lung illnesses and other ailments.

The first known documented use of mustard for culinary purposes dates back to the Romans in the first century CE. Records show that mustard seeds were ground into a paste before unfermented grape juice—known as *must*—was added, making it similar to the condiment that we know and love today. The Romans then brought mustard seeds to northern France, where monks began cultivating mustard plants in monasteries as early as the ninth century.

Centuries later, the yellow mustard we think of as classic arrived on the scene at the 1904 World's Fair in St. Louis, introduced by the R. T. French Company as "cream salad mustard." The French Brothers, George and Francis, added turmeric to their recipe to achieve that bright yellow shade, helping to make the condiment stand out a bit more than the typical brown version. It seemed to have worked: According to the *Encyclopedia of American Food and Drink*, 90 percent of hot dogs are eaten with mustard.

## Types of Mustard

- **Yellow:** smooth, slightly sweet, with a mild tang and a tinge of sharpness from the vinegar
- **Dijon:** creamy and smooth with a slight tang and spice
- **Whole grain:** seedy, earthy, and nutty
- **Fruit:** sweet-tart with a subtle mustard kick; texture can vary from chunky to smooth depending on the style
- **Hot:** pungent, smooth, with a sinus-clearing heat and sharp bite
- **Honey:** smooth, tangy, sweet, and mild
- **French:** mild, sweet, and slightly tangy
- **English:** smooth and sharp, with a hot, dry intensity
- **Chinese:** intense and nose-tingling
- **Alcoholic:** texture and flavor can vary depending on the fruit and booze used, but often malty, fruity, or oaky
- **Spicy brown:** bold, punchy, and slightly bitter with a lingering spice
- **Creole:** grainy and tangy, with a complex flavor of vinegar and horseradish

# WEST VIRGINIA SLAW DOGS

You'll find slaw dogs throughout the South, but West Virginia's version, which reportedly originated at Charleston's Stopette Drive-In, includes a meaty chili sauce for a nice contrast with the cool, crunchy slaw. Be sure to grate the cabbage for the slaw for optimal eating with (slightly) less mess; yellow mustard and diced onion hiding in between the chili and slaw add tang and bite.

**MAKES 8**

### For the chili sauce

2 tablespoons vegetable oil

1 small yellow onion, finely chopped

1 pound (454 grams) ground beef (ask your butcher for double-ground meat; that's usually the standard, but if not, just ask for it)

1 tablespoon chili powder

1 teaspoon onion powder

½ teaspoon sweet paprika

3 garlic cloves, minced

2 tablespoons tomato paste

2 tablespoons ketchup

1 tablespoon Worcestershire sauce

½ cup (125 ml) lager beer

Kosher salt and freshly ground black pepper to taste

### For the slaw

12 ounces (340 grams) shredded green cabbage

¼ cup (60 grams) mayonnaise

2 tablespoons white vinegar

2 teaspoons yellow mustard

¼ teaspoon celery salt

### For the hot dogs

8 hot dogs

8 hot dog buns

Yellow mustard

1 medium yellow onion, diced

**1. Make the chili sauce:** Heat the oil in a medium saucepan over medium-high heat. Add the onion and cook until soft, about 3 minutes, then stir in the ground beef. Cook until browned, about 5 minutes, then stir in the chili powder, onion powder, paprika, and garlic and cook for 2 minutes more. Stir in the tomato paste and cook for 2 minutes, then add the ketchup and Worcestershire sauce. Stir in the beer and 2 cups (500 ml) of water. Bring to a simmer and cook until thick, about 1 hour. Season with salt and pepper and keep warm.

**2. Make the slaw:** In a large mixing bowl, stir the cabbage, mayonnaise, vinegar, mustard, and celery salt until combined. Cover and chill until ready to serve.

**3. Make the hot dogs:** Grill the hot dogs (see page 5). Steam the buns (see page 7).

**4.** To assemble, place the hot dogs in buns and top with mustard, onion, and chili sauce, then finish with the coleslaw and serve.

# TEXAS TOMMY DOGS

Sorry, Texans, but the Lone Star State can't lay claim to this one. Invented in Pottstown, Pennsylvania, in the 1950s, the Texas Tommy features a hot dog split and stuffed with ripped slices of cheese, with the whole thing then wrapped in bacon and sautéed (it's also sometimes finished with mustard and ketchup). Think of it as a DIY cheese-filled hot dog; the bacon (use regular, not thick-cut) helps to hold it all together and should get perfectly crisp just as the molten cheese is starting to erupt from within.

**MAKES 8**

8 hot dogs
8 slices Cheddar cheese
8 slices bacon
8 hot dog buns
Ketchup
Mustard

**1.** Cut a slit, lengthwise, in each hot dog, taking care to not slice all the way through them. Working with one dog at a time, break up a slice of cheese and stuff it into the hot dog, then wrap the hot dog in a slice of bacon. Repeat with the remaining hot dogs, cheese, and bacon.

**2.** Heat a large nonstick skillet over medium heat. Working in batches, add the hot dogs and cook, rotating as needed, until the bacon is crisp and the cheese is *juuuust* starting to ooze out, about 6 minutes. Repeat with the remaining hot dogs, then transfer to a plate and keep warm.

**3.** Pan-fry the buns (see page 7).

**4.** To assemble, place a hot dog in each bun, top with ketchup and mustard, and serve.

# ALASKA DOGS

Hot dogs are a favorite street food throughout Alaska's largest city, Anchorage. The popular Yeti Dogs stand uses all sorts of meats for their franks, and reindeer is one of the most iconic. Reindeer meat may seem like enough of an oddity to those in the Lower 48, but what makes these dogs *really* stand out? It's the onions, browned and then glazed in Coca-Cola, that pair perfectly with the mildly gamy flavor of the reindeer. Top your wiener with anything you like, but to make it a true Alaska dog, you gotta add the Coca-Cola onions.

**MAKES 8**

2 tablespoons vegetable oil

1 pound (454 grams) yellow onions, thinly sliced

¾ cup (177 ml) Coca-Cola

8 reindeer sausages (available regionally or online), butterflied (see page 9)

8 hot dog buns

**1.** Heat the oil in a large skillet over medium-high. Add the onions and cook, stirring occasionally, until lightly golden, about 7 minutes. Add the Coca-Cola and cook, stirring occasionally, until the liquid has reduced, about 5 minutes. Keep warm until ready to use.

**2.** Cook your sausages and buns according to your desired preference, although we recommend grilling them (see pages 5 and 7).

**3.** To assemble, place the sausages in the buns, top with the onions and anything else you like, and serve.

# NEW YORK DOGS

New York City conjures up images of yellow taxis and subway cars, cartoonishly large rats munching on pizza, and, yes, the city's ubiquitous hot dog carts. Ominously nicknamed "dirty water" dogs, they are plucked straight from a tank of heated water right there in the cart and served in a steamed bun. (At more venerable stands like the Nathan's Famous in Coney Island, this all-beef masterpiece is griddled to perfection.) But wherever you get your New York–style dog, it should come with nothing more than spicy brown mustard and either sauerkraut or onions cooked in tomato sauce.

**MAKES 8**

**For the onions**

2 tablespoons vegetable oil

2 medium yellow onions, thinly sliced

¼ cup (60 grams) ketchup

½ teaspoon chili powder

½ teaspoon kosher salt

⅛ teaspoon ground cinnamon

**For the hot dogs**

8 hot dogs

8 hot dog buns

2 cups (284 grams) sauerkraut, warmed

Spicy brown mustard

**1. Make the onions:** Heat the oil in a medium skillet over medium heat. Add the onions and cook until lightly golden, about 10 minutes. Stir in the ketchup, chili powder, salt, and cinnamon. Add 1 cup (250 ml) of water and bring to a boil. Reduce the heat to maintain a simmer and cook, stirring occasionally, until the liquid has reduced and the sauce is thick, 8 to 10 minutes.

**2. Make the hot dogs:** Boil the hot dogs (see page 5). Steam the buns (see page 7).

**3.** To assemble, place a hot dog in each bun, then top with some of the onions and sauerkraut and drizzle with the mustard.

### All About the Onions

It's that tangy, oniony tomato sauce, first seen at the iconic Papaya King hot dog counter, that really sets a New York dog apart from other street dogs (well, that and a pigeon trying to rip it from your hand). Opened in 1932 by Greek immigrant Gus Poulos, Papaya King serves its signature all-beef, natural-casing hot dogs with spicy brown mustard and the tomatoey onions. (A refreshing papaya juice, inspired by the tropical fruit drinks that Poulos tried on a trip to Cuba back in the day, is also a must.)

# THE NATHAN'S HOT DOG EATING CONTEST

## A Competitive History

Legend has it that the very first hot dog eating competition took place outside of Nathan's Famous in Coney Island on July 4, 1916. There, four men were arguing among themselves about who was the most patriotic, and they determined that the only way to settle the matter was to see who could eat the most hot dogs. (Somehow it makes sense?)

It's unclear how many dogs the winner ate, or how many franks it takes to become the most patriotic, but the contest we know today officially began in the summer of 1972. The current record holder and perennial champion is Joey Chestnut, who wolfed down seventy-six hot dogs in 10 minutes in 2021. Miki Sudo holds the women's record with fifty-one franks in 10 minutes in 2024.

## The Rules of the Competition

- All competitors must be under contract with the International Federation of Competitive Eating.
- The competition is timed at 10 minutes (down from 12 minutes prior to 2008) for competitors to eat as many hot dogs and buns as they can.
- Competitors can add to their hot dogs but not take anything away. This means that toppings are allowed, although most do not partake. Most competitors use water or fruit juice to help them wash down their dogs or to dunk their hot dogs in. Dunking in liquid makes the hot dogs more malleable and thus easier to swallow.
- Messy eating can earn competitors a yellow card. Judges watch carefully to make sure the competitors are eating the entire hot dog.
- No puking (this is called a “reversal of fortune”).
- Any hot dog in a competitor’s mouth when time is up counts toward their total (but they do have to finish it).
- A tie for first place means a five-dog eat-off. First competitor to eat five hot dogs, wins. This happened in 2008 when Joey Chestnut ate five hot dogs in 50 seconds, beating Takeru Kobayashi.

# BALTIMORE HOT DOGS

You might be pleasantly surprised by how well two salty meats work together. Bologna is fried and then wrapped around a hot dog, which at first glance might seem a bit redundant, but if I've learned anything about hot dogs, the more meat the merrier. So, if you're ever in Charm City, head to Attman's Deli to get your hands on one of these gloriously greasy dogs.

**MAKES 8**

8 slices bologna
Vegetable oil, for cooking
8 hot dogs
8 hot dog buns
Sweet pickle relish
Spicy brown mustard
1 medium yellow onion, diced

**1.** Make a 1-inch slit in each piece of bologna so they don't curl when heated. Heat 1 tablespoon of the oil in a large skillet over medium heat. Working in batches, add some of the bologna slices in a single layer and cook, turning once, until golden on each side, 1 to 2 minutes. Transfer to a plate and keep warm. Repeat with the remaining slices of bologna, adding more oil as needed.

**2.** Pan-fry the hot dogs and buns (see pages 6 and 7).

**3.** To assemble, roll each hot dog in a slice of bologna and place in a bun. Top with the relish, mustard, and onion and serve.

***Pro Tip*** • Slather on some mayonnaise and add crushed potato chips to the top to make it more like a fried bologna sandwich!

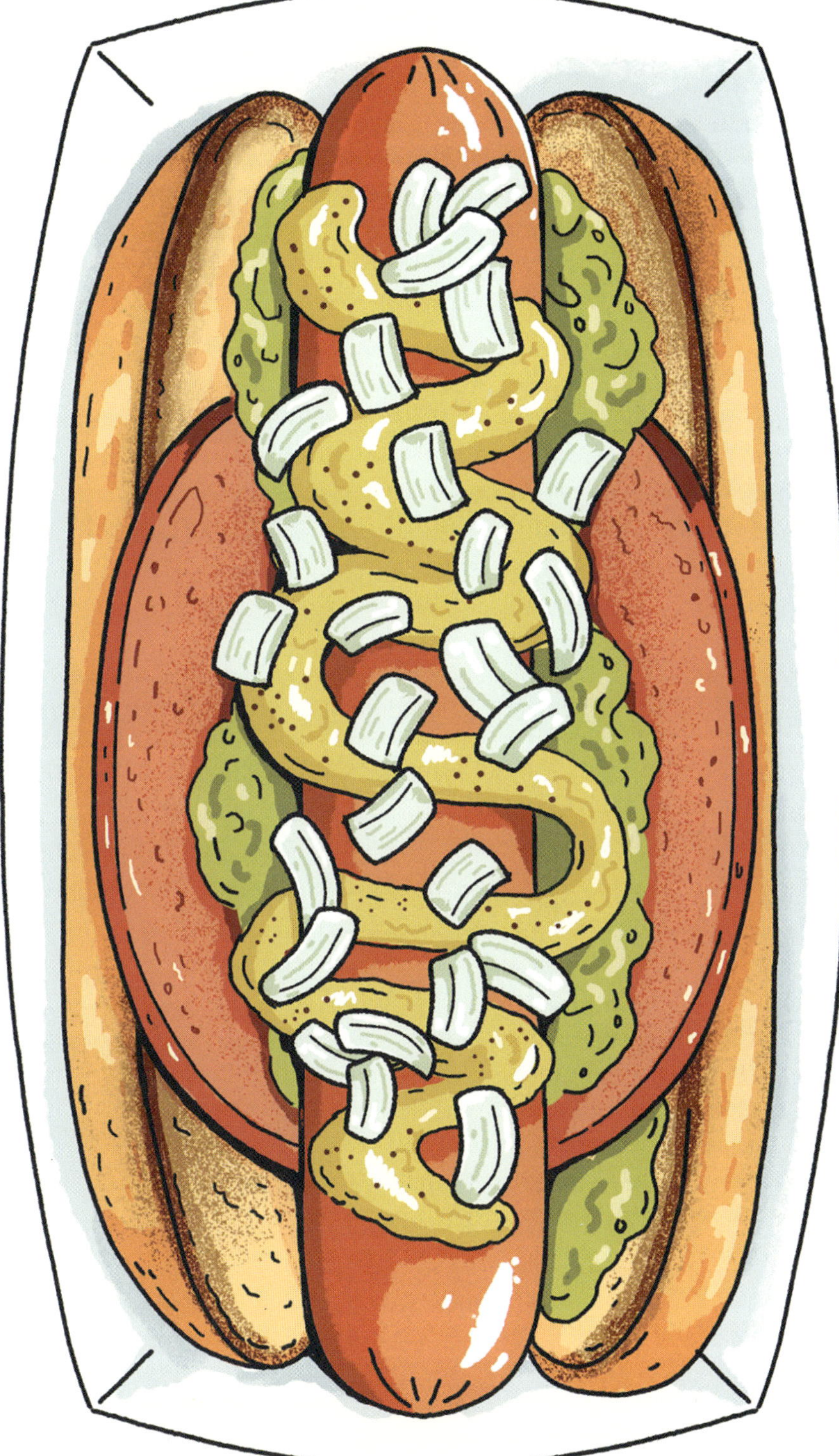

# RIPPERS

This beloved New Jersey frank is gloriously deep-fried, causing the casing to burst, or rip, giving the dog its slasher-movie-sounding name. It originated in 1928 at Rutt's Hut in Clifton, where they top the wrinkly wieners with a homemade mustard relish. You can also order your dog well-done, called a "weller," or very well-done, known as a "cremator."

**MAKES 8**

### For the relish

4 cups/1 pound (454 grams) finely chopped green cabbage (about ¾ head cabbage)

1 cup/5 ounces (142 grams) finely chopped carrot

1 cup/6 ounces (170 grams) finely chopped green bell pepper

1 cup/6 ounces (170 grams) finely chopped yellow onion

¼ cup (40 grams) kosher salt

1 cup (250 ml) white vinegar

2 cups (570 grams) granulated sugar

¾ teaspoon celery seeds

½ teaspoon mustard seeds

3 tablespoons all-purpose flour

1½ teaspoons ground turmeric

1 teaspoon dry mustard

2 tablespoons boiling water

### For the hot dogs

Neutral oil for deep-frying

8 hot dogs

8 hot dog buns

***Pro Tip*** • The relish at Rutt's Hut is iconic, so we encourage you to make it, although you could always use hot dog relish instead. The recipe here makes a lot; try preserving the leftovers in a sterilized quart canning jar and giving it as a host gift to friends—along with a pack of your favorite local hot dogs and a copy of this book—at your next gathering or party.

**1. Make the relish:** Combine the cabbage, carrot, bell pepper, onion, and salt in a large bowl and toss to combine. Allow to sit for 2 hours. Rinse the mixture thoroughly with cold water, drain and squeeze to remove excess liquid.

**2.** Transfer the vegetables, the vinegar, and 1 cup (250 ml) of water to a large saucepan. Cover and cook for 1 hour, then stir in the sugar, celery seeds, and mustard seeds.

**3.** In a small bowl, stir together the flour, turmeric, and dry mustard. Carefully stir the 2 tablespoons of boiling water into the flour mixture to form a paste. Add the paste to the simmering vegetable mixture and cook, stirring, until thick, about 5 minutes more. Cool completely before using.

**4. Make the hot dogs:** Deep-fry the hot dogs (see page 6), but if you want yours extra crispy, à la the Rutt's Hut cremator, keep it in the fryer a bit longer. Steam the buns (see page 7).

**5.** To assemble, place a hot dog in each bun, top with some relish, and serve.

# KANSAS CITY–STYLE DOGS

Known for barbecue with a thick, sweet sauce, Kansas City also knows how to hot dog. Slow-cooked pulled pork with homemade barbecue sauce is a classic topping, but if you've got some burnt ends from brisket, by all means use them instead. Make sure to finish with bread-and-butter pickles.

**MAKES 8**

**For the pulled pork and barbecue sauce**

1½ pounds (680 grams) boneless pork shoulder

Kosher salt to taste

1 cup (300 grams) ketchup

2 tablespoons apple cider vinegar

2 tablespoons granulated sugar

2 tablespoons light brown sugar

2 tablespoons molasses

1 tablespoon yellow mustard

1 teaspoon chili powder

1 teaspoon onion powder

½ teaspoon garlic salt

**For the hot dogs**

8 hot dogs

8 hot dog buns

Bread-and-butter pickles

**1. Make the pulled pork:** Heat the oven to 300°F. Season the pork all over with salt and place in a small baking dish. Cover with aluminum foil and cook until incredibly tender, about 3 hours. Remove from the oven and, using two forks, shred the meat.

**2. Make the barbecue sauce:** In a small saucepan, bring the ketchup, vinegar, sugars, molasses, mustard, chili powder, onion powder, garlic salt, and ½ cup (125 ml) of water to a boil over medium-high heat. Reduce the heat to maintain a simmer and cook, stirring occasionally, until thick, about 25 minutes.

**3.** Stir the barbecue sauce into the shredded meat and keep warm.

**4. Make the hot dogs:** Grill the hot dogs and buns (see pages 5 and 7).

**5.** To assemble, place a hot dog in each bun and top with some of the pulled pork. Shingle some pickles over the top and serve.

# What's the difference between CHILI and HOT DOG CHILI SAUCE?

Wait, there's a difference? That's right, the meat sauce you've enjoyed on chili dogs your whole life is different from the chili con carne that you eat in a bowl with shredded cheese and sour cream.

Hot dog chili sauce is thinner and typically doesn't contain beans, and the taste is usually a bit more tomatoey. Chili con carne, meanwhile, is often chunkier and spicier. The hot dog sauce has its roots in the Midwestern Coney dog and made its way across the United States primarily via Greek and Macedonian immigrants. (Between 1900 and 1919, the United States saw an influx of more than 340,000 Greek immigrants.) Upstate New York, Rhode Island, Ohio, Michigan, and beyond all have variations of the meat sauce designed for slathering on a hot dog.

Some hot dog purveyors make their meat sauce by double-grinding the meat for a smoother texture. To achieve the same effect at home, buy chuck steak and ask your butcher to grind it twice for you (or do it yourself if you have a meat grinder). Otherwise, you can try crumbling the meat with a potato masher or use an immersion blender to puree it a bit.

# DEPRESSION DOGS

Here's another classic dog born and bred in the Second City. Unlike its more dressed up cousin, the Chicago dog (page 19), this Great Depression–born wiener is steamed and served in a plain bun without poppy seeds and topped with yellow mustard, hot sport peppers, onions, and a mound of fries. Gene and Jude's, one of the most well-known spots to snag a Depression Dog in the Windy City, is often cited as the birthplace of the anti-ketchup ethos. The house rules clearly state, "No seats. No ketchup. No pretense. No nonsense." (Controversial!)

**MAKES 8**

- 1 bag (1 pound 10 ounces/737 grams) frozen classic French fries
- 8 hot dogs
- 8 hot dog buns
- Yellow mustard
- 1 large yellow onion, diced
- 16 sport peppers (purchasable in some regions and online)
- Sweet pickle relish (optional)

**1.** Cook the fries according to package directions.

**2.** Meanwhile, steam the hot dogs and buns (see pages 5 and 7).

**3.** To assemble, spread the inside of each bun with the mustard, then add a hot dog. Top each with some onion, two sport peppers, and some relish (if using). Finish with some fries and serve.

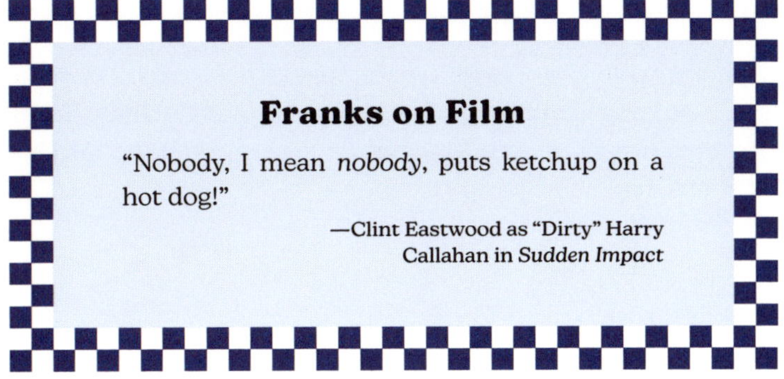

### Franks on Film

"Nobody, I mean *nobody*, puts ketchup on a hot dog!"

—Clint Eastwood as "Dirty" Harry Callahan in *Sudden Impact*

# SEATTLE DOGS

These beloved local wieners started popping up on the late-night scene in the city's popular Pioneer Square neighborhood during the heyday of grunge in the late 1980s and early 1990s. Vendors slather snappy natural casing hot dogs with cream cheese and serve them on a hardy bialy-style bun, but here we're using regular hot dog buns. Try using a piping bag to make schmearing the cream cheese on the soft bread a little easier.

**MAKES 8**

2 tablespoons vegetable oil

2 medium yellow onions, thinly sliced

Kosher salt to taste

8 hot dogs, butterflied (see page 9)

8 hot dog buns

8 ounces (225 grams) cream cheese, softened

Sriracha sauce

Spicy brown mustard

2 jalapeños, thinly sliced, for garnish

**1.** Heat the oil in a large skillet over medium-high. Add the onions and cook, stirring occasionally, until golden, about 10 minutes. Season with salt and keep warm.

**2.** Grill the butterflied hot dogs (see page 5). Grill the buns (see page 7).

**3.** Spoon the cream cheese into a piping bag or resealable bag and cut the tip off one corner.

**4.** To assemble, pipe some cream cheese onto each bun, then place a hot dog in each bun. Top with some of the onions. Drizzle with the sriracha and mustard, then garnish with the jalapeño slices and serve.

# Why We Eat Hot Dogs at BALLPARKS

There's no denying the lure of a hot dog at a baseball game. Despite its global appeal, the humble hot dog is a deeply American food, and pairing it with sports, baseball in particular, just fits.

There's nothing better than being outside in the sunshine and having someone throw you a hot dog wrapped in foil while you sit in stadium seats, beer or soda in hand. Maybe it has to do with the murky origin story of the hot dog (see page 2) or the fact that it's a handheld food best consumed outdoors, but franks and sports have become inextricably intertwined.

According to the National Hot Dog and Sausage Council (NHDSC), almost 20 million hot dogs are consumed each season at Major League games. Data also shows that Major League teams that sell the most hot dogs win the most games. "The right players on the field aren't the only ingredient of successful teams," said NHDSC President Eric Mittenthal. "It's clear that well-fed, enthusiastic fans drive winning, too, and no food makes fans happier at a ballgame than hot dogs and sausages."

Legend has it that Babe Ruth himself ate between twelve and eighteen hot dogs (and drank eight sodas) in one sitting between games of a doubleheader in 1925. (He also then collapsed and was hospitalized—don't be like the Babe.)

As renowned actor Humphrey Bogart once said, "A hot dog at the ballgame beats roast beef at the Ritz." Bogie might have been onto something there.

## Best Baseball Stadium Dogs

- **Boston Red Sox Fenway Frank:** Snappy franks are boiled and then grilled before getting wedged inside a classic New England–style bun (crustless on the sides with a split top).
- **Chicago Cubs Wrigley Dog:** An all-beef hot dog in a steamed bun that's dragged through the garden with the usual array of Chicago-style hot dog toppings.
- **Los Angeles Dodgers Dodger Dog:** A 10-inch hot dog that's soaked in beer then grilled. It's served with ketchup, mustard, onions, and sweet relish.
- **Baltimore Orioles Crab Mac n' Cheese Dog:** Creamy macaroni and cheese, lump crabmeat, and Old Bay seasoning dress up a hot dog; similar to the Chesapeake Bay dog (page 111).
- **Texas Rangers Boomstick Hot Dog:** Two feet long and loaded with jalapeños, cheese sauce, onions, and chili, it costs a not-exactly-cheap $32.96 at the time of this writing.
- **Atlanta Braves T.E.D. (The Everything Dog):** A footlong all-beef hot dog that's topped with queso, jalapeños, and tortilla chips, then sprinkled with popcorn and drizzled with barbecue sauce.
- **Arizona Diamondbacks Chicken Enchilada Dog:** An 18-inch chicken enchilada sausage on a telera roll (an oblong, fluffy, slightly sweet roll often used for tortas in Mexico) topped with queso blanco, enchilada sauce, pico de gallo, black olives, sour cream, and tortilla strips. Costs over $25 at time of writing—a steal compared to the Boomstick Hot Dog.

# PHILLY DOGS

Most people rightly associate Philadelphia with cheesesteaks, but the city has also produced a truly original spin on the hot dog. Debuting in 1895, the Philly Dog is still on the menu at Johnny's Hots in Fishtown, where they offer theirs with pepper hash—a veggie relish often served with seafood—and smashed, fried fish cakes, as here. Sure, it's an unusual spin on surf and turf, but if there's one lesson to learn from this book, it's that the most unusual hot dog combinations are sometimes the most surprisingly delightful.

**MAKES 8**

**For the pepper hash**

¼ cup (60 grams) granulated sugar

6 tablespoons (90 ml) apple cider vinegar

1 teaspoon kosher salt

½ teaspoon celery seeds

½ teaspoon mustard seeds

¼ teaspoon freshly ground black pepper

1 carrot, roughly chopped

1 small green bell pepper, stemmed, seeded, and roughly chopped

1 small red bell pepper, stemmed, seeded, and roughly chopped

½ medium green cabbage, cored and roughly chopped

**For the sausages**

8 hot sausages, split

8 hoagie-style buns

8 frozen round breaded fish cakes

Spicy brown mustard

Diced white onion

**1. Make the pepper hash:** In a medium saucepan, combine the sugar, vinegar, salt, celery seeds, mustard seeds, and black pepper. Cook over medium heat, stirring, until the sugar and salt are dissolved, then remove from the heat and cool completely.

**2.** Place the carrot and bell peppers in the bowl of a food processor and pulse until finely chopped. Alternatively, coarsely grate the carrots and finely chop the bell peppers. Add to a large bowl and stir in the cabbage. Add the cooled vinegar mixture and toss to combine. Cover and refrigerate for at least 2 hours.

**3. Make the sausages:** Grill the sausages (see page 5). Toast buns in a pan (see page 7).

**4.** Cook the fish cakes according to the package instructions and keep warm.

**5.** To assemble, place a sausage in each bun. Break the fish cakes in half and top each sausage with two halves. Top with mustard and onion, finish with the hash, and serve.

## Philly Fish Facts

Cheesesteaks date back to the 1930s, when brothers Pat and Harry Olivieri opened the famous Pat's King of Steaks. The fish cake dog, however, has even deeper Philly roots; Abe Levis is credited with creating it in 1895, when franks (and fried fish) were popular and cheap working-class meals.

# ITALIAN HOT DOGS

This New Jersey masterpiece originates from Jimmy Buff's in Newark, circa 1932. It's topped with a potato, pepper, and onion mixture with a smear of mustard inside the bread. (Though this dog is commonly served on bread made from leftover pizza dough, we opted for torpedo rolls—basically a long sub roll—for convenience.) Sometimes, you'll find the potatoes cut into rounds, but here we went with chunks, similar to what you'll see at Dickie Dee's in Bloomfield, New Jersey.

**MAKES 8**

- 4 tablespoons vegetable oil, plus more for deep-frying
- 1½ pounds potatoes, peeled, and cut into 1-inch pieces
- 1 medium green bell pepper, stemmed, seeded, and sliced
- 1 medium red bell pepper, stemmed, seeded, and sliced
- 1 medium yellow onion, sliced
- 1 teaspoon Italian seasoning
- Kosher salt and freshly ground black pepper to taste
- 8 hot dogs
- 8 torpedo rolls
- Spicy brown mustard
- Ketchup (optional)

**1.** Heat the oil in a large cast-iron skillet over medium heat. Add the potatoes and cook until golden, about 25 minutes. Using a slotted spoon, transfer the potatoes to a medium bowl.

**2.** Add the bell peppers and onion to the skillet and stir in more oil if needed. Cook, stirring, until soft, about 10 minutes. Return the potatoes to the skillet and stir in the Italian seasoning and cook for 2 minutes more. Season with salt and black pepper and keep warm.

**3.** Deep-fry the hot dogs (see page 6). Steam the rolls in the microwave (see page 7).

**4.** To assemble, spread mustard inside each bun, then add the hot dogs. Top each with some of the potato mixture, add ketchup if you're feeling frisky, and serve.

2
International Styles

# PERROS CON TODO

### Venezuela

Venezuelans really do put everything on their hot dogs, just as "perros con todo" suggests, and this bad boy gets a trio of flavorful sauces. The corn sauce is sweet and smooth, while guasacaca—reminiscent of guacamole—is rich and creamy, and the garlic sauce is herbaceous and bright. Three sauces might seem like a lot, but each brings something different to the bun. Potato chips, avocado, Gouda, cabbage, and onion add a fun array of textures to help balance the whole thing out.

**MAKES 8**

**For the corn sauce**

5 tablespoons (75 grams) mayonnaise

3 tablespoons cream cheese

2 tablespoons vegetable oil

1 tablespoon yellow mustard

1 can (15.5 ounces/439 grams) sweet corn kernels, rinsed and drained

Kosher salt to taste

**For the guasacaca**

½ cup (125 ml) white vinegar

3 medium avocados, halved, peeled, and pitted

1 garlic clove

1 small bunch cilantro, roughly chopped

1 small yellow onion, roughly chopped

½ green bell pepper, stemmed, seeded, and roughly chopped

Kosher salt to taste

**For the garlic sauce**

4 garlic cloves, minced

1 teaspoon kosher salt

¾ cup (225 grams) mayonnaise

3 tablespoons minced cilantro

1½ tablespoons fresh lime juice

Granulated sugar to taste

**For the hot dogs**

8 hot dogs

8 hot dog buns

Diced yellow onion

Finely chopped green cabbage

Sliced avocado

Salsa rosada (page 80)

Ketchup

Yellow mustard

Shredded Gouda cheese

Crushed potato chips

**1. Make the corn sauce:** Place the mayonnaise, cream cheese, oil, mustard, and corn in the bowl of a food processor or blender and puree until smooth. Strain in a fine-mesh strainer, pressing to extract as much sauce as possible. Discard the solids. Season with salt and set aside until ready to use.

**2. Make the guasacaca:** Place the vinegar, avocados, garlic, cilantro, onion, and bell pepper in the bowl of a food processor or blender and puree until smooth. Season with salt and set aside until ready to use.

**3. Make the garlic sauce:** Place the garlic cloves on a cutting board and sprinkle with the salt. Using the flat side of a knife, smash it into a paste, then transfer it to a small bowl. Stir in the mayonnaise, cilantro, and lime juice, then season with sugar. Set aside until ready to use.

**4. Make the hot dogs:** Boil the hot dogs (see page 5) and steam the buns (see page 7).

**5.** To assemble, place each hot dog in a bun, as well as some diced onion, cabbage, and avocado. Drizzle on each of the sauces, plus the salsa rosada, ketchup, and mustard. Sprinkle with cheese and potato chips and serve.

# HOT DOG FLOWERS

## China

These beautiful pastries can be found in many Chinese bakeries, particularly throughout Hong Kong. We'll use the same fluffy dough as that of the sausage-filled Czech klobásník (page 112), but instead of leaving it whole like a pig in a blanket, the hot dog–filled pastry is sliced and twisted to form the shape of a flower before being topped with sesame seeds and scallions. Once baked, the flowers are glazed with sugar syrup to give them a nice sheen.

**MAKES 8**

2¾ cups (430 grams) all-purpose flour

1 teaspoon kosher salt

½ cup (125 ml) whole milk

¼ cup (60 grams) plus 2 tablespoons granulated sugar

2¼ teaspoons active dry yeast

4 tablespoons (56 grams) unsalted butter, melted

1 large egg yolk plus 1 large egg

8 hot dogs

2 scallions, thinly sliced

1 teaspoon black sesame seeds

1 teaspoon toasted white sesame seeds

**1.** Line two sheet pans with parchment paper. In a medium bowl, stir together the flour and salt and set aside.

**2.** Heat the milk and ½ cup (125 ml) of water to 115°F. Transfer to the bowl of a stand mixer fitted with a dough hook attachment along with 2 tablespoons of the sugar and the yeast. Let sit until foamy, about 10 minutes, then add in the butter and the egg yolk. Add the flour and salt and mix at medium speed until a soft, smooth dough forms. Divide the dough into 8 even pieces. Roll each piece of dough into a ball and place on one of the prepared sheet pans. Cover with a kitchen towel and let rise in a warm place until doubled in size, about 1 hour.

**3.** In a small saucepan, combine the remaining sugar and ¼ cup (60 ml) of water. Heat over medium heat until sugar is dissolved. Set the syrup aside until ready to use.

*(continues)*

**4.** Heat the oven to 400°F. Working with one ball of dough at a time on a clean work surface, roll the dough into a 5½-inch by 4½-inch oval and place a hot dog on top. Roll up into a log, sealing the edges.

**5.** Form the hot dogs into flower shapes. Using kitchen scissors or a sharp knife, make 5 to 6 equal cuts across the hot dog log and through the dough underneath, taking care not to cut all the way through, leaving a thin strip of dough and dog at the bottom to hold the "petals" together. Carefully rotate each cut petal segment outward so the sliced hot dog faces up in a pinwheel shape.

**6.** Place the pastries on the prepared sheet pans and let rise for 15 minutes.

**7.** Meanwhile, in a small bowl, beat the whole egg, then mix in the scallions.

**8.** Brush the egg over the pastry and, using your fingers, dab the scallions all over, then sprinkle with the sesame seeds. Try not to get any scallions or seeds on the hot dogs (just to keep them looking cute). Bake, rotating the pans halfway through, until golden, about 15 minutes. Brush with the syrup and cool slightly before serving.

# SHUCOS

## Guatemala

*Shuco* means "dirty" in Spanish, which is just another way to say that this hot dog gets messy. Usually made with a combination of either chorizo or longaniza sausage and hot dogs, shucos are typically grilled over charcoal, then sliced and served with boiled cabbage, guacamole, ketchup, mayo, and mustard—with the option of adding pico de gallo or queso fresco, because why not? Live a little!

**MAKES 8**

### For the guacamole

2 avocados, halved, peeled, and pitted

1 teaspoon kosher salt

1 lime, juiced (2 to 3 tablespoons)

### For the cabbage

8 ounces (225 grams) green cabbage, thinly sliced

Kosher salt to taste

### For the hot dogs

4 hot dogs

4 chorizo or longaniza sausages, about 3 to 4 ounces (100 g) each

8 hot dog buns

Ketchup

Mayonnaise

Mustard

Habanero peppers, stemmed, seeded, and thinly sliced (optional)

**1. Make the guacamole:** In a medium bowl, mash the avocados with the salt and lime juice. Cover and refrigerate until ready to use.

**2. Make the cabbage:** Place the cabbage in a large saucepan and add water to cover. Bring to a boil over high heat, then reduce the heat to maintain a simmer. Cook until soft, about 5 minutes, then drain. Season with salt and set aside.

**3. Make the hot dogs:** Grill the hot dogs and sausages (see page 5) and grill the buns (see page 7). Transfer the meats to a cutting board and thinly slice, then divide among the buns. Top each with the guacamole, cabbage, ketchup, mayonnaise, mustard, and sliced peppers, if using.

# A SAUSAGE (and Hot Dog) TUTORIAL

Yes, this book focuses on hot dogs, but there is indeed an entire edible universe of tubular meats out there for us to enjoy. As a quick refresher, the key difference between dogs and sausages is that the meat in a hot dog is more finely ground and generally more mildly spiced than that of a sausage. (And despite their differences, you can definitely use hot dogs in place of sausages in many recipes, and vice versa. After all, a hot dog is technically a cooked sausage!)

So, without further ado, let's review this wide world of hot dogs and their close cousins, sausages.

- **Bratwurst:** A mildly spiced German sausage typically made from pork, although beef or veal can also be used.
- **Knockwurst:** Also a German sausage, it's similar to bratwurst, though usually with stronger spice, particularly garlic, pepper, and paprika, which gives it an orange hue. In Germany, it's spelled *knackwurst* (*knack* meaning "snap"). When the sausages arrived in the American Midwest, their spelling was changed to *knockwurst*.
- **Polish sausage (kielbasa):** Pork sausages that can either be fresh or smoked and usually have a strong marjoram or coriander flavor. (*Kielbasa* means "sausage" in Polish.)
- **Half-smokes:** Found in and around Washington, DC, these usually feature more coarsely ground meat and are typically made from half pork and half beef in a natural casing.
- **Red hots or hot links:** Found around the western and upstate New York cities of Rochester, Syracuse, and Buffalo, these dogs are also called Texas hots. They're made from beef, pork, or a combination

of the two in a natural pork casing. You can also find red hots in North Carolina, and in Georgia, they're typically found on the scrambled dog (see page 128).

- **White hots:** Also popular around the Rochester area, white hots (sometimes called porkers) are made from a combination of uncured and unsmoked pork, beef, or veal. The lack of smoking is how it maintains its pale complexion. They also usually contain less veal and less sodium than a typical hot dog. Back in the 1920s, white hots were often made out of butchering leftovers and were known as poor-man hot dogs, although today they're made with the same meats as other hot dogs.
- **Red snappers:** Found predominantly around Maine, these bright, neon-red beef and pork hot dogs come in a natural casing, W. A. Bean & Sons have been making them for more than 150 years.
- **Footlongs:** Despite the name, footlongs aren't necessarily 12 inches long. These bun-dwarfing guys are popular throughout Scandinavia (see pages 84 and 86).
- **Kosher:** Kosher hot dogs do not contain pork, and the beef or poultry used to make them has been slaughtered according to Jewish law.
- **Chorizo:** This pork sausage is either fresh in Mexican cuisine or smoked in Spanish and is usually spicy.
- **Longaniza:** A long Spanish sausage that is usually made from pork; ingredients vary depending on the region.
- **Vegetarian:** These guys are free from animal products and typically contain soy, wheat, or pea protein, while their casings are made from cellulose or another plant-based ingredient.

# PØLSE I LOMPER

## Norway

Norway *loves* hot dogs; the average Norwegian eats around 100 each year. The word *pølse* means sausage, and *lompe* is a tortilla-style wrap made from potatoes. If you're a little skeptical about shrimp salad on a hot dog, trust that it works. The creaminess of the mayonnaise and sour cream pairs well with the salty hot dog. And the shrimp? Just consider it Scandinavian surf and turf.

**MAKES 8**

### For the shrimp salad

6 ounces (170 grams) peeled and steamed baby shrimp, roughly chopped

3 tablespoons sour cream

1 tablespoon mayonnaise

1 tablespoon minced dill

1 small rib celery, finely chopped

Zest of 1 lemon, plus 1 tablespoon fresh lemon juice

Kosher salt to taste

### For the lomper

1 pound (454 grams) russet potatoes, scrubbed clean

6 tablespoons (45 grams) all-purpose flour, plus more for dusting

6 tablespoons (45 grams) fine rye flour

½ teaspoon kosher salt

### For the hot dogs

8 hot dogs

1 small yellow onion, finely chopped

Crispy fried shallots

**1. Make the shrimp salad:** In a medium bowl, combine the shrimp, sour cream, and mayonnaise. Stir in the dill and celery, plus the lemon zest and juice. Season with salt and refrigerate until ready to use.

**2. Make the lomper:** Place the potatoes in a medium saucepan and add water to cover. Bring to a boil over high heat, then lower the heat and simmer until the potatoes are tender, about 25 minutes. Drain and cool slightly, then peel.

*(continues)*

**3.** Put the potatoes through a ricer into a large bowl, then stir in the flours and salt. Mix until smooth. Divide the dough into eight balls, about 2 ounces (56 grams) each. Heat a large cast-iron skillet or griddle over medium heat.

**4.** Working with one ball of dough at a time on a floured work surface with a floured rolling pin, gently roll the dough into 6- to 7-inch circles. Note: The dough can stick quite a bit. Roll the dough out slowly and a little at a time, taking care to kind of reform it into a circle as you go. The dough is forgiving and easy to work with, so feel free to patch any holes you might get or reform the shaggy edges to make it into more of a circle. Brush off any extra flour as best you can with a pastry brush.

**5.** Carefully transfer the lompe to the skillet and cook, turning once, until golden and puffed on both sides, 2 to 3 minutes per side. Wrap it in a clean kitchen towel to keep warm and repeat with the remaining balls of dough.

**6. Make the hot dogs:** Boil the hot dogs (see page 5).

**7.** To assemble, top each lompe with a hot dog, some shrimp salad, raw onions, and crispy shallots and serve.

## Spud History

Potatoes arrived in Norway via the Americas in the fifteenth century. Norwegians were skeptical of the tuber at first, referring to it as "the devil's fruit" because it grew underground. It wasn't until they understood the many health benefits of potatoes that they began adding them more frequently to their diet and became certified spud-lovers. Yet another benefit: Potatoes go really *really* well with hot dogs.

# PYLSA

## Iceland

This celebrated hot dog is found throughout Iceland—most famously at the Bæjarins Beztu Pylsur chain of stands in Reykjavik. It's topped with remoulade, sweet mustard (known as pylsusinnep), both crispy and raw onions, and ketchup. The snappy, beer-braised pylsa dogs feature a triple threat of lamb, pork, and beef.

**MAKES 8**

### For the pylsusinnep

¼ cup (30 grams) dry mustard

2 tablespoons light beer

1 tablespoon honey

1 tablespoon white wine vinegar

1 teaspoon ketchup

½ teaspoon kosher salt

### For the remoulade

½ cup (150 grams) mayonnaise

1 tablespoon minced capers

1½ teaspoons white wine vinegar

1 teaspoon Dijon mustard

1 teaspoon minced fresh dill

1 teaspoon minced fresh parsley

### For the hot dogs

1 can (12 ounces/375ml) light beer

8 hot dogs

8 hot dog buns

1 medium yellow onion, diced

Ketchup

Crispy fried shallots

**1. Make the pylsusinnep:** In a large bowl, stir together the dry mustard and beer, then add the honey, vinegar, ketchup, and salt. Cover and refrigerate at least 1 hour, preferably overnight.

*(continues)*

**2. Make the remoulade:** In a small bowl, combine the mayonnaise, capers, vinegar, and mustard. Stir in the herbs. Cover and refrigerate until ready to use.

**3. Make the hot dogs:** Pour the beer and 2 cups (500 ml) of water into a medium saucepan. Bring to a simmer over medium-low heat, then add the hot dogs and cook until plumped and heated through, 4 to 5 minutes. Steam the buns (see page 7).

**4.** To assemble, place each dog in a bun and top with some raw onions, the pylsusinnep, remoulade, ketchup, and fried shallots.

***Pro Tip*** • Are you just not quite mustard-obsessed enough to make your own pylsusinnep? Don't sweat it. Fortunately, through the wonders of the internet, the iconic condiment (with its adorable illustration of a cute hot dog wearing a chef's hat) is available for purchase.

# EL COMPLETO ITALIANO

## Chile

Is it Chilean? Italian? Something else entirely? One thing's for sure: It's a hot dog—'nuff said. You'll find several well-topped variations of the "completo" hot dog throughout Chile; the original contains sauerkraut and salsa americana (a mix of pickled carrots, cucumbers, and onions). But arguably the most popular is the completo Italiano, topped with mashed avocado, diced tomatoes, and a drizzle of mayonnaise—colors that are meant to represent the Italian flag.

**MAKES 8**

2 large ripe avocados, halved, peeled, and pitted

Juice of 1 lime

Kosher salt to taste

8 hot dogs

8 hot dog buns

2 medium tomatoes, diced

Mayonnaise

**1.** In a medium bowl, mash the avocado until mostly smooth. Season with the juice from the lime and salt. Set aside until ready to use.

**2.** Steam the hot dogs (see page 5) and the buns (see page 7).

**3.** To assemble, place a hot dog in each bun and top with some tomatoes. Add some of the avocado mixture, then drizzle on the mayonnaise and serve.

# CACHORRO QUENTE

## Brazil

Here's another South American hot dog with a *lot* going on! Brazilians make a tomatoey sauce to heat these dogs, but the fun doesn't stop there. The franks are then topped with a trinity of condiments (mayonnaise, ketchup, and mustard) as well as grated Parmesan cheese, crispy potato sticks, and sometimes steamed peas and corn kernels. It's true what they say: Sometimes more *is* more.

**MAKES 8**

2 tablespoons vegetable oil

1 medium onion, thinly sliced

1 medium green bell pepper, stemmed, seeded, and thinly sliced

3 garlic cloves, minced

½ teaspoon dried oregano

½ teaspoon dried thyme

1 can (15 ounces/425 grams) tomato sauce

8 hot dogs, butterflied (see page 9)

Kosher salt and freshly ground black pepper to taste

8 hot dog buns

Ketchup

Mayonnaise

Mustard

Grated Parmesan cheese

Potato sticks

**1.** Heat the oil in a large saucepan over medium heat. Add the onion and cook, stirring occasionally, until soft, 4 to 5 minutes. Add the bell pepper and cook until soft, 5 to 6 minutes. Stir the garlic and cook until fragrant, 1 to 2 minutes, then stir in the oregano, thyme, tomato sauce, and 1 cup (250 ml) of water. Bring to a boil over high heat, then reduce the heat to maintain a simmer. Cook until thick, about 15 minutes.

**2.** Add the hot dogs and cook 5 minutes more. Season with salt and pepper and keep warm.

**3.** To assemble, place each hot dog in a bun and top with some of the sauce. The buns aren't usually heated, but feel free to toast or heat them (see page 7). Drizzle on the ketchup, mayonnaise, and mustard, then sprinkle on some Parmesan cheese. Top with the potato sticks and serve.

# PERROS CALIENTES

### Colombia

According to one of my Colombian friends, "Pineapple sauce is like ketchup for Colombians." And slathering it on a hot dog is a must-try. Perros calientes are also topped with salsa rosada, a sauce made from a mixture of mayonnaise and ketchup, and finished with crushed potato chips. This sweet-and-salty hot dog will truly make you rethink sticking to only savory toppings. Side note: Perros calientes can often be found topped with hard-boiled quail eggs, as well!

**MAKES 8**

**For the pineapple sauce**

¼ cup (60 grams) granulated sugar, plus more to taste

½ teaspoon kosher salt

1 can (20 ounces/567 grams) crushed pineapple

Juice of 1 lime (about 3 tablespoons)

**For the salsa rosada**

¼ cup (60 grams) mayonnaise

3 tablespoons ketchup

Kosher salt and freshly ground black pepper to taste

**For the hot dogs**

8 hot dogs buns

8 hot dogs

Mayonnaise

Ketchup

Potato chips

**1. Make the pineapple sauce:** In a small saucepan, combine the sugar, salt, pineapple, and lime juice. Cook over medium heat, stirring occasionally, until thick, about 30 minutes. Season with more sugar. Cool completely. Puree in a blender for a smoother sauce if desired.

**2. Make the salsa rosada:** In a small bowl, stir together the mayonnaise and ketchup. Season with salt and pepper, then set aside until ready to use.

**3. Make the hot dogs:** Boil the hot dogs (see page 5). Steam the buns (see page 7).

**4.** To assemble, place each hot dog in a bun and top with the pineapple sauce and salsa rosada. Add a squirt of both mayonnaise and ketchup. Crush some potato chips over the top of each and serve.

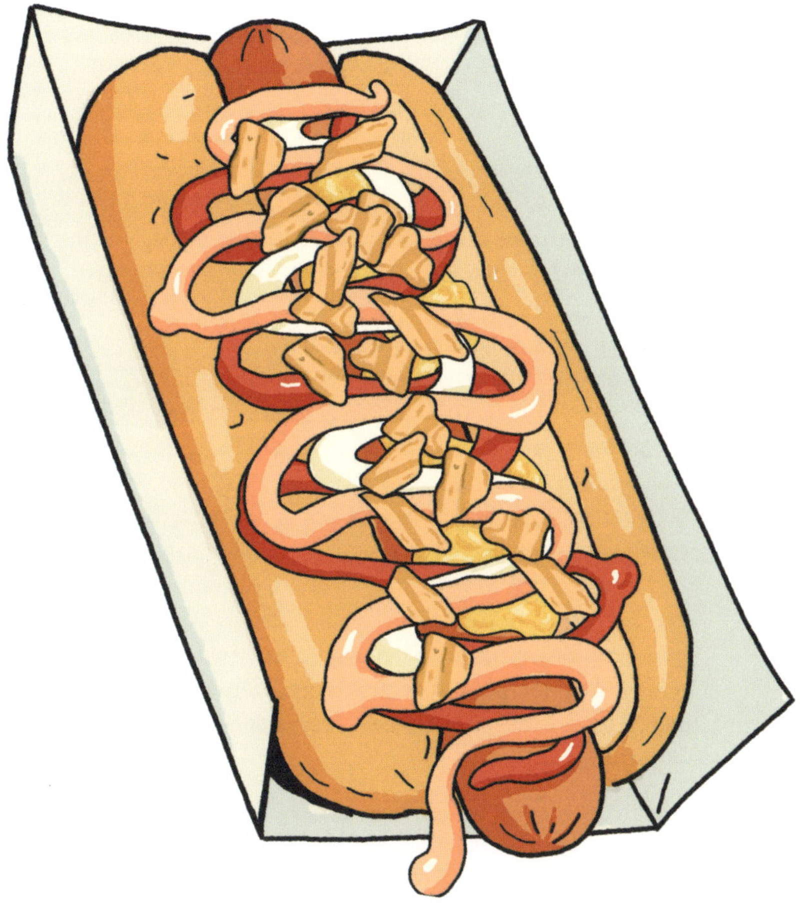

# Why Do We Call Them HOT DOGS, Anyway?!

Many of us have heard the nasty claim that hot dogs got their name because, well, they supposedly at one time contained the meat from man's best friend. This unpleasant (and false!) sentiment has lingered since the nineteenth century, appearing in newspapers and songs of the time. But the real reason that we came to call our beloved, processed tube-o-meat in a bun a "hot dog" remains quite hazy.

One of the most widely accepted origin stories for the naming of the dog comes from New York's Polo Grounds, home of the Giants baseball team. The year was 1901. The month, April. The weather? Cold and rainy. Legend has it that concessionaire extraordinaire Harry M. Stevens had stocked up on loads of ice cream and sodas in anticipation of a sunny spring day. When the weather failed him, he told his son, Frank (no pun intended), to run out to the many German shops in the neighborhood to "buy up all of those German sausages you can, those long dachshund sausages" as well as some long buns and mustard. Before you know it, they were selling hot dogs at the ballpark, calling them "red hots" because "those people were freezing. They'd want something hot."

According to the unconfirmed story, famed cartoonist T. A. Dorgan was in the press box that day, and when it came time for him to submit his cartoon of the game to the *New York Journal*, the image that he allegedly created was that of a vendor slinging the dogs. Unable to properly spell *dachshund* (can you blame him?), he captioned his illustration "Get your hot dogs!" instead.

## OTHER NAMES FOR HOT DOGS

- Wieners or weenies
- Frankfurters or franks
- Red hots
- Glizzies
- Footlongs
- Coneys
- Naked dogs
- Snags (Australia)
- Bangers
- Tube steaks

A likelier origin story does in fact stem from the suspicion of the dubious ingredients in German sausages all those years ago. The first known instance of the term *hot dog* being used to refer to a sausage in a bun was printed in a Yale University humor magazine in the 1890s. Campus lunch wagons began to be referred to as "dog wagons," thanks to a poem that appeared in the *Yale Record* in October 1895:

*Tis dogs' delight to bark and bite,*
*Thus does the adage run.*
*But I delight to bite the dog*
*When placed inside a bun.*

"Dog wagon" led to "hot dog," and from there the term spread to other colleges and newspapers and into popular culture.

Meanwhile, we get the hot dog synonyms *frankfurter* or *frank* from Frankfurt-style sausages, and *wiener* or *wien* from Vienna-style sausages. Both Germany and Austria lay claim to inventing the hot dog; it seems the only completely verifiable fact is that hot dogs are the world's greatest food.

# THE HALV SPECIAL

## Sweden

This iconic Gothenburg hot dog feels a bit like bangers and mash in bun form. Sometimes served with a squirt of both ketchup and mustard but almost always topped with crispy onions, the Halv Special can be doubled in size, which turns it into the Hel Special, by using two hot dogs instead of one. Similar to the Danish rød pølse (page 86), this Swedish wonder almost always comes with a cold glass of Pucko, a chocolate milk drink that is a national favorite.

**MAKES 8**

### For the mashed potatoes

1½ pounds (680 grams) russet potatoes, peeled and cut into 1-inch pieces

Kosher salt to taste

6 tablespoons (170 grams) unsalted butter

6 tablespoons (90 ml) whole milk

Freshly ground black pepper to taste

### For the hot dogs

8 hot dogs

8 hot dog buns

Ketchup

Mustard

Crispy fried onions

**1. Make the mashed potatoes:** Place the potatoes in a medium saucepan and cover with water. Season generously with salt. Bring to a boil and cook until the potatoes are soft, about 12 minutes, then drain. Transfer the potatoes back to the pan along with the butter and milk. Use a potato masher to mash the potatoes. Season with salt and pepper and keep warm.

**2. Make the hot dogs:** Boil the hot dogs (see page 5). Steam the buns (see page 7).

**3.** To assemble, place a hot dog in each bun, then drizzle with ketchup and mustard. Top each with some mashed potatoes, sprinkle with some crispy fried onions, and serve.

# RØD PØLSER

## Denmark

Denmark's rød pølser ("red sausages") are long, thin, pork-based hot dogs that are dyed bright red. Traditional toppings include a creamy remoulade and sweet fresh pickles, as well as minced onion and crispy shallots. Like Sweden's Halv Special, (see page 84), serve this dog with cold chocolate milk (sounds weird, sure, but when it works, it works). If you can't find rød pølse, any hot dog that is longer than the bun will work just fine (bonus points if it's red).

**MAKES 8**

### For the sweet pickles

1 cup (250 ml) apple cider vinegar

½ cup (120 grams) granulated sugar

1 teaspoon kosher salt

¼ cup (60 ml) warm water

1 English cucumber, thinly sliced

### For the remoulade

¾ cup (200 grams) mayonnaise

1½ tablespoons fresh lemon juice

1½ tablespoons minced capers

1½ tablespoons minced fresh parsley

1½ tablespoons whole grain mustard

Kosher salt to taste

### For the hot dogs

8 Copenhagen street dogs (røde pølser)

8 hot dog buns

Ketchup

Spicy mustard

1 medium yellow onion, diced

Store-bought fried shallots

**1. Make the sweet pickles:** In a medium bowl, whisk together the vinegar, sugar, and salt with the warm water until the sugar and salt have dissolved. Add the sliced cucumber and let sit for at least 30 minutes at room temperature.

**2. Make the remoulade:** In a small bowl, stir together the mayonnaise, lemon juice, capers, parsley, and mustard. Season with the salt and set aside until ready to use.

*(continues)*

**3. Make the hot dogs:** Boil the hot dogs (see page 5) and toast the buns in a pan (see page 7).

**4.** To assemble, place a hot dog in each bun and drizzle on some ketchup and mustard. Dollop on some remoulade, then sprinkle with the fresh onions and the fried shallots. Add a layer of the sweet pickles and serve.

## Frank Fact

Back in the day, Danish hot dog vendors added red dye to let people know they were buying day-old dogs for a fraction of the cost of freshies. But it isn't just the red color that makes rod pølser stand out; the Danes smoke their dogs with beechwood and add spices like allspice, nutmeg, and cardamom to the meat mixture. For even more flavor, many hot dog stands, called pølsevogne, boil their dogs in broth rather than water.

# CURRYWURST

## Germany

Typically made with bratwurst and served with fries, this popular Berlin street food is slathered with a curry ketchup sauce. Here, we vary things by using hot dogs and a combination of tomato sauce and tomato paste for the sauce.

**MAKES 4**

- 4 tablespoons olive oil
- 1 small yellow onion, finely chopped
- 2 tablespoons light brown sugar
- 2 tablespoons tomato paste
- 1 tablespoon mild curry powder, plus more for serving
- 1 teaspoon sweet paprika
- ¾ cup (177 ml) vegetable stock
- 2 tablespoons apple cider vinegar
- 1 can (8 ounces/227 grams) tomato sauce
- Kosher salt to taste
- 8 hot dogs, thinly sliced into coins
- French fries, for serving

**1.** Heat 2 tablespoons of the oil in a large skillet over medium heat. Add the onion and cook until soft, about 5 minutes. Add the brown sugar and cook, stirring occasionally, until the onion is golden, about 5 minutes. Stir in the tomato paste, curry powder, and paprika and cook 2 minutes, then stir in the stock, vinegar, and tomato sauce. Cook, stirring occasionally, until thick, 12 to 15 minutes. Transfer to a blender and puree until smooth. Season with salt and keep warm.

**2.** Heat the remaining 2 tablespoons of oil in a large skillet over medium-high heat. Add the hot dogs and cook, stirring occasionally, until golden all over, about 5 minutes.

**3.** To assemble, divide the hot dogs among four plates and drizzle with the sauce. Sprinkle with curry powder and serve with fries.

# SOSIS BANDARI

## Iran

Hailing from southern Iran, this classic and flavorful street food (whose name means "port sausage" in Farsi) typically comes in sandwich form. Heaped with potatoes and peppers reminiscent of a hash, as in New Jersey's Italian dogs (page 60) or even the cachorro quente in Brazil (page 78), the sosis bandari is loaded with spices for extra punch. While an arugula salad with crumbled feta is by no means traditional, it's a welcome addition to help lighten and brighten this classic.

**MAKES 8**

- 7 tablespoons (105 ml) olive oil
- 1½ pounds (680 grams) russet potatoes, cut into ½-inch pieces
- 8 hot dogs, cut into ½-inch-thick rounds
- 1 green bell pepper, stemmed, seeded, and diced
- 1 yellow onion, diced
- 1 teaspoon ground cumin
- ½ teaspoon ground turmeric
- ½ teaspoon hot paprika
- 3 tablespoons tomato paste
- Kosher salt and freshly ground black pepper to taste
- 1 cup (225 grams) plain full-fat yogurt
- 2 ounces (55 grams) crumbled feta
- Zest and juice from 2 lemons
- 2 ounces (55 grams) baby arugula
- 1 cup (15 grams) fresh parsley leaves
- ½ cup (10 grams) fresh dill sprigs
- 1 baguette

**1.** Heat 4 tablespoons of the oil in a large skillet over medium. Add the potatoes and cook, stirring occasionally, until golden all over, about 25 minutes.

**2.** Move the potatoes over to one side of the skillet, then add an additional 1 tablespoon of oil and the hot dogs and cook until the dogs are golden and plump, about 3 minutes. Stir in the bell pepper and onion and cook until soft, about 4 minutes more, then stir in the cumin, turmeric, and paprika and cook for 1 minute. Stir in the tomato paste and cook for 2 minutes, then add ¼ cup (60 ml) of water and cook until thick, 1 to 2 minutes more. Season with salt and black pepper and keep warm.

**3.** In a small bowl, combine the yogurt with the feta. Stir in the lemon zest and season with salt and pepper. Refrigerate until ready to use.

**4.** In a medium bowl, toss the arugula with the remaining 2 tablespoons of oil and the herbs. Squeeze in the juice of the lemons and season with salt and pepper.

**5.** To assemble, cut the baguette crosswise evenly into four pieces, then slice each piece in half lengthwise. Spread the yogurt mixture on the insides of the slices of bread, then top the bottom slices with the sosis bandari and the herb salad. Finish with the top half of the baguette and serve.

# CHORIPAN

## Argentina

Argentinians are known for their fantastic grilled meats, and this chorizo-based masterpiece is typically served as an appetizer before a traditional barbecue, or asado. (Anyone who serves dressed-up hot dogs as a prelude to even more meat is doing something right.) So fire up the grill and throw on the chorizo and baguettes, then drizzle with herby, vinegary chimichurri sauce to brighten things up. And don't forget a bit of tomato salsa to finish it all off.

**MAKES 8**

### For the salsa

1 large tomato, diced

½ small sweet onion, diced

1 tablespoon olive oil

1 teaspoon red wine vinegar

Kosher salt to taste

### For the chimichurri

¾ cup (46 grams) finely chopped fresh parsley

⅓ cup (78 ml) olive oil

¼ cup (60 ml) red wine vinegar

2 teaspoons kosher salt

½ teaspoon hot red pepper flakes

2 garlic cloves, finely grated

Freshly ground black pepper to taste

### For the sausages

8 chorizo sausages, 3 to 4 ounces (100 g) each

Olive oil

2 baguettes, cut into eight chorizo-length pieces

**1. Make the salsa:** In a medium bowl, stir together the tomato and onion with the olive oil and vinegar. Season with salt and set aside.

**2. Make the chimichurri:** In a small bowl, mix the parsley with the olive oil, vinegar, salt, red pepper flakes, and garlic. Season with the black pepper and set aside.

**3. Make the sausages:** Grill the chorizo (see page 5). When charred all over, transfer the sausages to a cutting board and butterfly them (see page 9). Place the butterflied chorizo, split-side down, back on the grill and cook until cut sides are charred, about 2 minutes more.

**4.** Brush the insides of the bread with olive oil and grill until charred, about 2 minutes.

**5.** To assemble, place the chorizo into the grilled baguettes. Top with the salsa and chimichurri and serve.

# KHANOM TOKYO

## Thailand

These sweet, thin pancakes are a popular Thai street food (no, Khanom Tokyo isn't Japanese, despite the name). They're often filled with sweet custard, but you can also find them with savory fillings. Here, they're sprinkled with ground pork and egg before being rolled around a hot dog. Mini dogs would work well, although using half a hot dog is fine, too.

**MAKES 8**

### For the pancake batter

1 cup (138 grams) all-purpose flour

1 tablespoon granulated sugar

2 teaspoons baking powder

1 teaspoon kosher salt

1 cup (250 ml) whole milk

2 tablespoons unsalted butter, melted

1 teaspoon pure vanilla extract

1 large egg

### For the filling

1 tablespoon vegetable oil

8 ounces (225 grams) ground pork

1 tablespoon minced cilantro roots or stems

1 garlic clove, minced

Kosher salt to taste

2 large eggs, beaten

Soy sauce to taste

Ground white pepper to taste

4 hot dogs, halved

**1. Make the pancake batter:** In a medium bowl, mix together the flour, sugar, baking powder, and salt. In a small bowl, whisk together the milk, butter, vanilla, and egg. Whisk the milk mixture into the dry ingredients and set aside for 20 minutes.

**2. Make the filling:** Heat the oil in a medium skillet over medium-high. Add the pork and cook, breaking it up with a wooden spoon, until golden, about 3 minutes. Add the cilantro roots and garlic and cook until fragrant, 1 minute more. Season with salt and set aside until ready to use.

**3. Make the hot dogs:** Boil the hot dogs (see page 5). Keep warm until ready to use.

*(continues)*

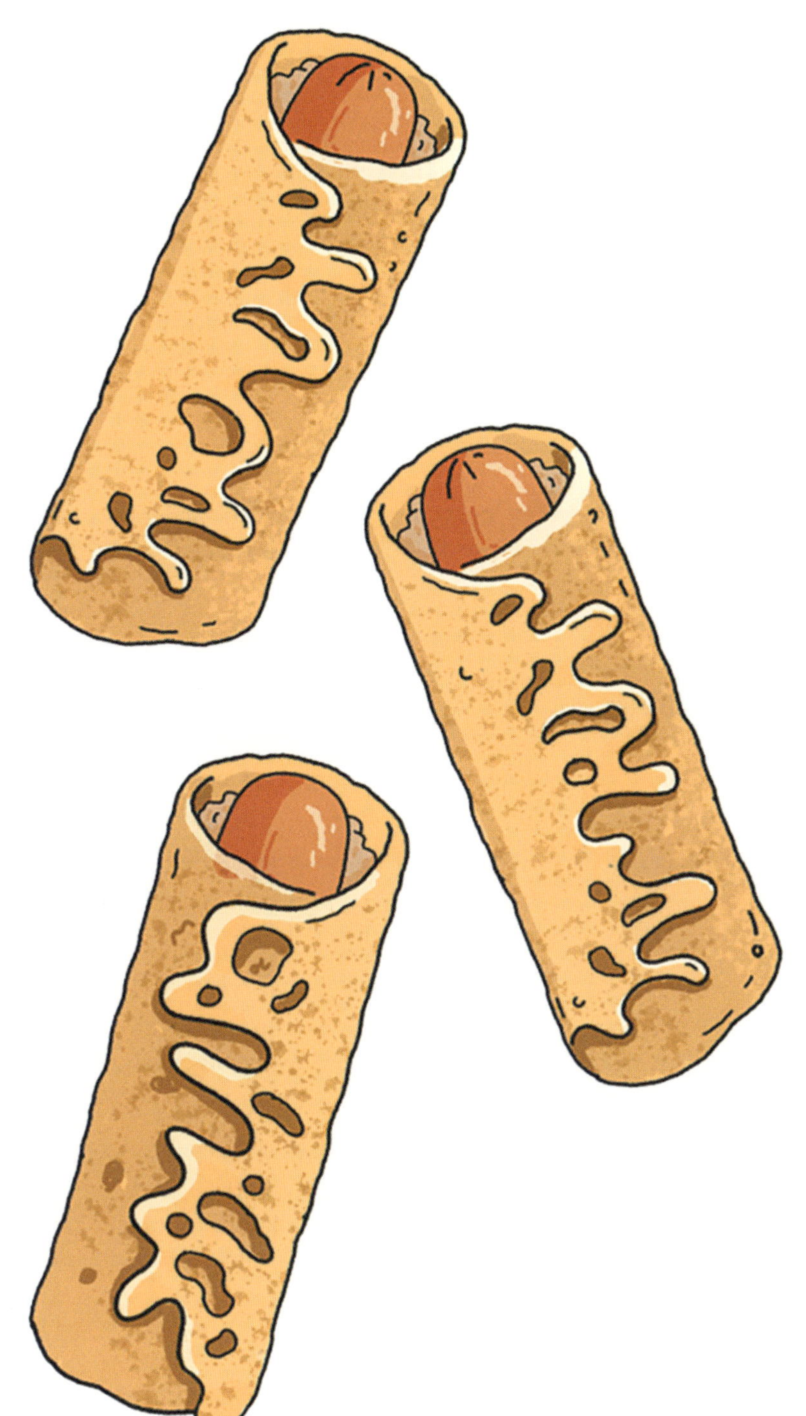

**4. Cook the pancakes:** Place one-third of the pancake batter in a squeeze bottle or piping bag. Heat a small nonstick skillet over medium. Drizzle a couple dots of the oil into the skillet, then ladle in 2 to 3 tablespoons of batter and spread it into a thin layer over half of the skillet. Drizzle some of the batter from the squeeze bottle onto the other half of the skillet, making squiggly lines that connect to the other half of batter. (Alternatively, you can spoon the batter over, however, it won't come out as thin.)

**5.** Spoon about 1 tablespoon of the beaten egg onto the pancake, then dollop on 1½ to 2 tablespoons of the pork filling. Drizzle on some soy sauce, then sprinkle on some white pepper. Cook until the underside of the pancake is lightly golden, about 2 minutes.

**6.** To assemble, add a hot dog half and roll up. Keep warm. Repeat with the remaining batter and filling, adding more oil to the skillet as needed. Serve warm.

# MONTREAL STEAMIES

## Canada

Move over, poutine. This Canadian wonder, called *steamé* in French and popular throughout Montreal, consists of a steamed dog and bun dressed up with finely chopped raw cabbage (seasoned simply with salt, pepper, oil, and vinegar), plus yellow mustard and diced onion. You can also opt for relish, although it does tend to make the bun a bit soggy. But, hey, it's your hot dog!

**MAKES 8**

8 ounces (225 grams) grated or finely chopped green cabbage

1 tablespoon olive oil

1 tablespoon white wine vinegar

Kosher salt and freshly ground black pepper to taste

8 hot dogs

8 hot dog buns

1 large yellow onion, diced

Yellow mustard

**1.** In a large bowl, toss the cabbage with the oil and vinegar and season with salt and pepper.

**2.** Steam the hot dogs (see page 5) and buns (see page 7).

**3.** To assemble, place a hot dog in each bun, then top with some onion and mustard. Finish with the cabbage and serve.

***Pro Tip*** • Prefer not to steam your steamie? Try the toastie (*toasté*), where the dog and bun are cooked on a flattop.

3
Wild &
Original

# TACO TUESDAY DOGS

Forget the old "is a hot dog a sandwich?" debate. I dare to ask, *could a hot dog be a taco?* (It's not so crazy: In Guatemala, they serve their hot dogs in corn tortillas, where they're known as mixtas.) Here we top dogs with a spiced ground beef mixture and the Taco Tuesday fixings of your dreams.

**MAKES 8**

**For the ground beef filling**

2 tablespoons vegetable oil

1 pound (450 grams) ground beef

1½ teaspoons garlic salt

1½ teaspoons ground cumin

1½ teaspoons onion powder

1½ teaspoons sweet paprika

1 teaspoon ground coriander

½ teaspoon cayenne

Kosher salt and freshly ground black pepper to taste

**For the tacos and hot dogs**

8 hard taco shells

8 (6-inch) flour tortillas

1 can (16 ounces/453 grams) refried beans

8 hot dogs

8 ounces (225 grams) shredded Mexican cheese blend

1 cup (90 grams) shredded iceberg lettuce (about ¼ head)

2 medium tomatoes, diced

½ cup (120 grams) sour cream

**1. Make the filling:** Heat the oil in a large skillet over medium-high heat. Add the ground beef and cook, breaking up the pieces with the back of a wooden spoon, until browned, about 5 minutes. Add the garlic salt, cumin, onion powder, paprika, coriander, and cayenne and cook for 2 minutes. Add ½ cup (120 ml) of water and bring to a boil. Cook 2 minutes more, then season with salt and pepper and keep warm.

**2. Make the tacos and hot dogs:** Heat the oven to 325°F. Place the hard taco shells in one layer on a sheet pan. Wrap the flour tortillas in aluminum foil. Place the sheet pan and wrapped tortillas in the oven and bake until the hard shells are crisp, 6 to 7 minutes, and the flour tortillas are warmed through. Keep warm.

**3.** Meanwhile, in a small saucepan, warm the refried beans over medium heat, stirring occasionally, until warmed through, about 8 minutes. Keep warm.

**4. Make the hot dogs:** Cook the hot dogs using whatever method you choose (see pages 5–6).

**5.** To assemble, spread about 2 tablespoons of the refried beans onto one side of each flour tortilla. Place the hot dog in the hard shell and place it on one half of the flour tortilla. Fold the other half over the exposed side of the hard shell (the refried beans act as a glue to hold the two shells together). Top the hot dog with the ground beef mixture, then sprinkle with some of the shredded cheese. Top with lettuce, tomatoes, and a dollop of sour cream, and serve.

# Is a HOT DOG a SANDWICH?

One of the most controversial questions in the vast world of hot doggery—and, yes, there are many—goes like this: *Is a hot dog a sandwich?* Let's review the facts:

## *Fact*

Merriam-Webster defines **'san(d)-ˌwich** as:

> **a:** two or more slices of bread or a split roll having a filling in between
> **b:** one slice of bread covered with food

Now think about the seam of a hot dog bun. You'd probably consider it to be a split roll, much like the bread one would use to make a hoagie or a sub.

## *Fact*

In 2011, New York State declared that the hot dog was a sandwich and therefore subject to sales tax.

## *Fact*

Consider this exchange between Stephen Colbert and Justice Ruth Bader Ginsburg in 2018:

> **Colbert:** Is a hot dog a sandwich?
>
> **Ginsburg:** You're asking me? Well, you tell me what a sandwich is, and then I'll tell you if a hot dog is a sandwich.
>
> **Colbert:** A sandwich is two pieces of bread with almost any type of filling in between, as long as it's not more bread.

**Ginsburg:** You say two pieces of bread. Does that include a roll that's cut open but still not completely?

**Colbert:** That's the crux. You've gotten [it] immediately. See this is why you're on the Supreme Court. That gets immediately to the question: Does the roll need to be separated into two parts? Because a sub sandwich—a sub is not split, and yet it is a sandwich.

**Ginsburg:** Yes.

**Colbert:** So then a hot dog is a sandwich?

**Ginsburg:** On your definition, yes, it is.

## Fact

Some might argue that, because a sandwich by definition requires that bread be involved, then a hot dog is not a sandwich since, well, you don't *need* bread to enjoy a hot dog.

## Fact

According to the Cube Rule of Food, you can determine the identity of a food based on the placement of the starch. For example, if the starch is only on the bottom, it's toast, whereas a sandwich has starch on the top and bottom. A taco has starch on the top, bottom, and sides. Therefore, it would appear that a hot dog is actually a taco.

We're not even going to get into an argument about whether a taco is a sandwich. That's for another book.

## Conclusion

Who the hell knows?

# FANCY LOBSTER ROLL DOGS

Honestly, nothing is better than a lobster roll in the summer—aside from a hot dog, of course. Combine the two and you have yourself the perfect handheld summer snack. Rather than mixing lobster meat with mayo or melted butter, try crème fraîche (or sour cream) for a richer flavor. And to top it all off? Caviar, of course . . . plus potato chips, because this is a humble ole hot dog, after all.

**MAKES 8**

- 2 pounds (900 grams) cooked lobster meat, diced
- 3 tablespoons crème fraîche
- 1½ teaspoons minced fresh chives, plus more for garnish
- Zest and juice from 1 lemon
- Kosher salt and freshly ground black pepper to taste
- 8 hot dogs
- 4 tablespoons (56 grams) unsalted butter, at room temperature
- 8 split-top brioche buns
- Potato chips
- As much caviar as you can afford

**1.** In a medium bowl, combine the lobster meat with the crème fraîche and chives. Add lemon zest and juice to taste. Season with salt and pepper and refrigerate until ready to use.

**2.** Pan-fry the hot dogs (see page 6). Butter the outsides of the buns and heat a large nonstick skillet over medium heat. Working in batches if necessary, add the buns to the skillet and cook, turning once, until lightly golden on both sides, about 2 minutes.

**3.** To assemble, place a hot dog in each bun and top each with some lobster mixture. Crush some potato chips over the top and add a dollop of caviar—as much as you feel like. Sprinkle with additional chives and serve.

# CHICKPEA CURRY DOGS

Inspired by a recipe from Madhur Jaffrey, this simple, flavorful chickpea curry is obviously terrific on its own, but when added to a hot dog, it very well might be—dare I say it—even better. The sweetness from mango chutney helps tame a bit of the heat from the curry, and boondi (a typical Indian snack made from chickpea flour) adds nice crunch. Hot dog buns work well here, but naan would be a great option, too.

**MAKES 8**

**For the curry**

3 garlic cloves, roughly chopped

3 small green chiles, roughly chopped

1½-inch piece ginger, peeled and roughly chopped

1 medium plum tomato

2 tablespoons vegetable oil

1 small red onion, minced

¼ cup (15 grams) minced fresh cilantro leaves and tender stems

1½ teaspoons ground coriander

1 teaspoon ground cumin

¼ teaspoon chili powder

¼ teaspoon ground turmeric

1 can (15.5 ounces/439 grams) chickpeas, rinsed and drained

Kosher salt to taste

**For the hot dogs**

8 hot dogs

8 hot dog buns or naan

Mango chutney

Boondi

**1. Make the curry:** In the bowl of a small food processor, blend the garlic, chiles, and ginger with 1 to 2 tablespoons of water until a paste forms.

**2.** Grate the tomato on a box grater, discarding the skin, and set aside until ready to use.

**3.** Heat the oil in a medium saucepan over medium-high heat. Add the onion and cook until lightly golden, about 5 minutes. Add the ginger-garlic paste along with the cilantro, coriander, cumin, chili powder, and turmeric. Cook until fragrant, 1 to 2 minutes, then stir in the grated tomato, chickpeas, and ½ cup (125 ml) of water. Reduce the heat to maintain a simmer and cook, uncovered and stirring occasionally, until thick, 8 to 10 minutes. Season with salt and keep warm.

**4. Make the hot dogs:** Cook the hot dogs and buns using whatever method you choose (see pages 5–7).

**5.** To assemble, place a hot dog in each bun and top with some chutney and curry. Garnish with the boondi and serve.

# SAUSAGE SIZZLE DOGS

Here's a creation inspired by the sausage sizzle, a type of community event or fundraiser common throughout Australia and New Zealand, at which hot dogs or sausages are served on white bread with grilled onions and sauces. To ramp up the Oceanian flavor, this version includes a classic Aussie and Kiwi staple: Vegemite, the thick, dark, salty paste made from leftover brewers' yeast extract. Okay, Vegemite (and its close cousin, Marmite) is a bit of an acquired taste—a little goes a long way.

**MAKES 8**

- 2 tablespoons vegetable oil
- 4 medium onions, thinly sliced
- 1 tablespoon Vegemite
- ¾ cup (177 ml) beer
- 8 hot dogs
- 8 slices white bread
- Ketchup

**1.** Heat the oil in a large skillet over medium-high heat. Add the onions and cook, stirring, until lightly golden, 7 to 8 minutes. Add the Vegemite and let soften for about 1 minute, then add the beer. Cook, stirring to break up the Vegemite, until the beer has reduced and the Vegemite has dissolved, about 2 minutes more.

**2.** Grill the hot dogs (see page 5).

**3.** To assemble, place each hot dog on a slice of bread and top with some of the onions. Drizzle on some ketchup and serve.

### Frank Fact

In Australia, corn dogs are called Dagwood dogs, dippy dogs, or Pluto pups depending on the region.

# A Brief History of
# HOT DOG BUNS

Among the many lures of the hot dog are its affordability and portability. No utensils required (for the most part) and, often enough, no plate needed either. But just as the hot dog's etymology evades us, conclusively identifying the hot dog bun's inventor seems forever out of reach.

One fun—and probably apocryphal—origin story asserts that German immigrant Antoine Feuchtwanger, who sold hot sausages on the streets of St. Louis, Missouri, in the 1880s, gave out white gloves to his customers to avoid burning their hands and to keep them clean. But as people weren't returning the gloves, Feuchtwanger asked his brother-in-law, a baker, to create split rolls to hold the sausages. His creation went on to appear at the 1904 World's Fair in St. Louis (or at the 1893 World's Fair in Chicago . . . or at a baseball game in 1883, depending on who's telling the story).

Some evidence shows the hot dog bun had been around since at least 1843, but whichever way you slice it, hot dogs were put into buns so that the working person could grab a frank from a street cart and eat it on the go. For most city dwellers in the early twentieth century, their place of work was far from their home and they needed something quick to eat on their lunch break. The hot dog was the perfect meal. (It still is, if we're being honest.)

No matter who invented it, the hot dog bun marked a clear shift to the modern-day hot dog. It's truly part of the fabric of American life, and its affordability has made it a food for everyone.

# PINEAPPLE SALSA HOT DOGS

We know from the delicious pineapple sauce slathered atop the Colombian Perros Calientes (page 80) that pineapple can and *should* be added to other hot dogs. Here it's mixed with creamy avocado and fresh lime zest and juice, plus a vinegary purple slaw. It's light, slightly sweet, and refreshing—the perfect counterbalance to the salty dog.

**MAKES 8**

**For the slaw**

8 ounces (225 grams) thinly sliced red cabbage

3 tablespoons white vinegar

Kosher salt to taste

**For the salsa**

12 ounces (340 grams) pineapple, finely diced

1 tablespoon minced fresh cilantro, plus sprigs for garnish

1 avocado, halved, peeled, pitted, and cut into ¼-inch pieces

1 small shallot, finely chopped

Zest and juice of 1 lime

8 hot dogs

8 hot dog buns

**1. Make the slaw:** In a large bowl, toss the cabbage and vinegar and let sit for 10 to 15 minutes until lightly pickled, then season with the salt and set aside.

**2. Make the salsa:** In a medium bowl, stir together the pineapple, cilantro, avocado, shallot, and lime zest and juice. Set aside.

**3. Make the hot dogs:** Cook the hot dogs and buns using whatever method you choose (see pages 5–7).

**4.** To assemble, place a hot dog in each bun, then add some slaw. Top with pineapple salsa, garnish with cilantro sprigs, and serve.

# CHESAPEAKE BAY HOT DOGS

Marylanders like me will add jumbo lump crabmeat to just about anything. Let's give hot dogs the Chesapeake Bay treatment with a mixture of crab, corn, vinegar, and Old Bay, just like a good crab boil. Grilling the corn adds a nice smokiness to the sweet kernels and crabmeat, while crushed potato chips on top add texture.

**MAKES 8**

- 2 ears corn, shucked
- 8 ounces (225 grams) jumbo lump crabmeat
- 4 tablespoons (56 grams) unsalted butter, melted
- 2 tablespoons apple cider vinegar
- 2 teaspoons Old Bay seasoning
- 1½ teaspoons minced fresh parsley
- Kosher salt and freshly ground black pepper to taste
- 8 hot dogs
- 8 hot dog buns
- Potato chips, preferably Old Bay or crab-flavored (but plain are fine if that's all you got!)

**1.** Light a grill and cook the corn, turning as needed, until tender and charred all over, about 14 minutes. Alternatively, turn the oven on broil and place the corn on a sheet tray. Broil, turning as needed, until charred all over, about 15 minutes. Let cool slightly, then cut the kernels from the cob.

**2.** In a large bowl, stir together the corn kernels, crabmeat, butter, vinegar, Old Bay seasoning, and parsley. Season with salt and pepper and set aside.

**3.** Cook the hot dogs and buns using whatever method you choose (see pages 5–7).

**4.** To assemble, place each hot dog in a bun and top with the corn and crab mixture. Crumble the potato chips over the tops and serve.

# KLOBÁSNÍKS

Like its sweeter, fruit-filled cousin, the kolache, this breakfast pastry was adapted by Czech immigrants who settled in Texas. The savory dough is usually wrapped around kielbasa sausages along with any other fillings (here, we're rolling with jalapeño and Cheddar). They're kind of like really big pigs in a blanket—how could that ever be a bad thing?

**MAKES 8**

- 2¾ cups (430 grams) all-purpose flour
- 1 teaspoon kosher salt
- ½ cup (125 ml) whole milk
- 2 tablespoons granulated sugar
- 2¼ teaspoons active dry yeast
- 4 tablespoons (56 grams) unsalted butter, melted
- 1 large egg yolk plus 1 large egg
- 8 slices Cheddar cheese
- 4 jalapeños, thinly sliced
- 8 hot dogs
- 1 tablespoon poppy seeds

***Pro Tip*** • You can also use this same enriched dough to make Chinese Hot Dog Flowers (page 66).

**1.** Stir the flour and salt together in a medium bowl.

**2.** Heat the milk and ½ cup (125 ml) water to 115°F. Transfer to the bowl of a stand mixer fitted with a dough hook along with the sugar and yeast. Let sit until foamy, about 10 minutes, then stir in the butter and the egg yolk. Add the flour and salt and knead on medium speed until a soft, smooth dough forms. Divide the dough into eight even pieces. Roll each piece of dough into a ball and place on a parchment paper–lined sheet pan. Cover with a towel and let rise in a warm place until doubled in size, about 1 hour.

*(continues)*

**3.** Heat the oven to 400°F. Working with one ball of dough at a time, roll the dough into a 5-inch circle and place a slice of cheese on top. Place 4 slices of jalapeño on the edge of the circle closest to you and place a hot dog on top. Roll up the hot dog in the dough, pressing and sealing the edge as best you can. Place on the sheet pan and repeat with the remaining dough balls, cheese, jalapeño slices, and hot dogs.

**4.** In a small bowl, beat the egg. Brush the klobásníks with the beaten egg and sprinkle with the poppy seeds. Let rest for 15 minutes.

**5.** Bake the klobásníks, rotating sheet pan halfway through, until golden and puffed, about 15 minutes. Cool for 5 minutes, then serve.

# A Brief History of the WIENERMOBILE

German immigrants Oscar F. Mayer and Gottfried Mayer began their meat and cold-cut operation in 1883 on Chicago's North Side. It wasn't until 1936, however, that Oscar's nephew Carl came up with the (frankly) ingenious idea of a 13-foot-long hot dog–shaped car to cruise the streets of Chi-Town advertising the brand, and the beloved Oscar Mayer Wienermobile was born. The now-iconic hot dog on wheels expanded its territory to the East Coast and Midwest, but in 1940, it was retired from the road due to gas rationing during World War II.

Fear not, Oscar Mayer fans, for in 1952, five new Wienermobiles triumphantly returned to the streets, and this time each stretched to an impressive 22 feet. Six years later, these marvels of engineering would incorporate buns into their brilliant design.

In 1977, a dark year in the Wienermobile's history, Oscar Mayer retired the fleet from service, choosing to instead focus their advertising budget on television. But the Wienermobile was only down, not out. In 1988, a fleet of six new 23-footers decked out with microwaves, refrigerators, cellphones, and stereos came onto the scene.

Exciting new Wienermobile tech continues apace, and each year, thousands of applicants apply to be one of twelve to drive around the country in the six current Wienermobiles. (Once selected, this cadre of elite drivers train at Hot Dog High.) You can even locate the Wienermobile nearest to you via an online tracker.

# HOT DOG FLAUTAS

Originating in Mexico, flautas are corn tortillas rolled up around a variety of fillings, then fried. We're topping ours with traditional ingredients, but go wild and add a drizzle of your favorite condiments like ketchup, mustard, and shredded cheese.

**MAKES 8**

8 (6-inch) corn tortillas
8 hot dogs
Vegetable oil for frying
Kosher salt to taste
Crema
Jalapeño sauce (page 16, optional)
Guacamole (page 69, optional)
Shredded lettuce
Crumbled cotija cheese
Diced tomatoes
Chopped white onion
Lime wedges

**1.** Heat a heavy medium skillet over medium heat. Working with one tortilla at a time, cook the tortilla, turning once, until soft and pliable, about 1 minute. Keep warm by wrapping in a kitchen towel. Repeat with the remaining tortillas. Alternatively, microwave the tortillas, one at a time, for about 10 seconds each and keep warm in a towel.

**2.** Place a hot dog on the bottom half of a tortilla. Roll it up tightly, like a cigar, and secure with a toothpick. Repeat with remaining hot dogs and tortillas.

**3.** Line a plate with paper towels. Heat 2 inches of the vegetable oil in a large, heavy saucepan until a deep-fry thermometer reads 350°F. Working in batches, carefully add the flautas to the oil and fry, turning as needed, until golden and crisp, about 4 minutes. Transfer to a paper towel–lined plate and season with salt.

**4.** To assemble, remove the toothpicks from the flautas, then line them up on a platter. Drizzle on the crema, then the jalapeño sauce and guacamole, if using. Sprinkle with the lettuce, cotija, tomatoes, and onion. Serve with lime wedges.

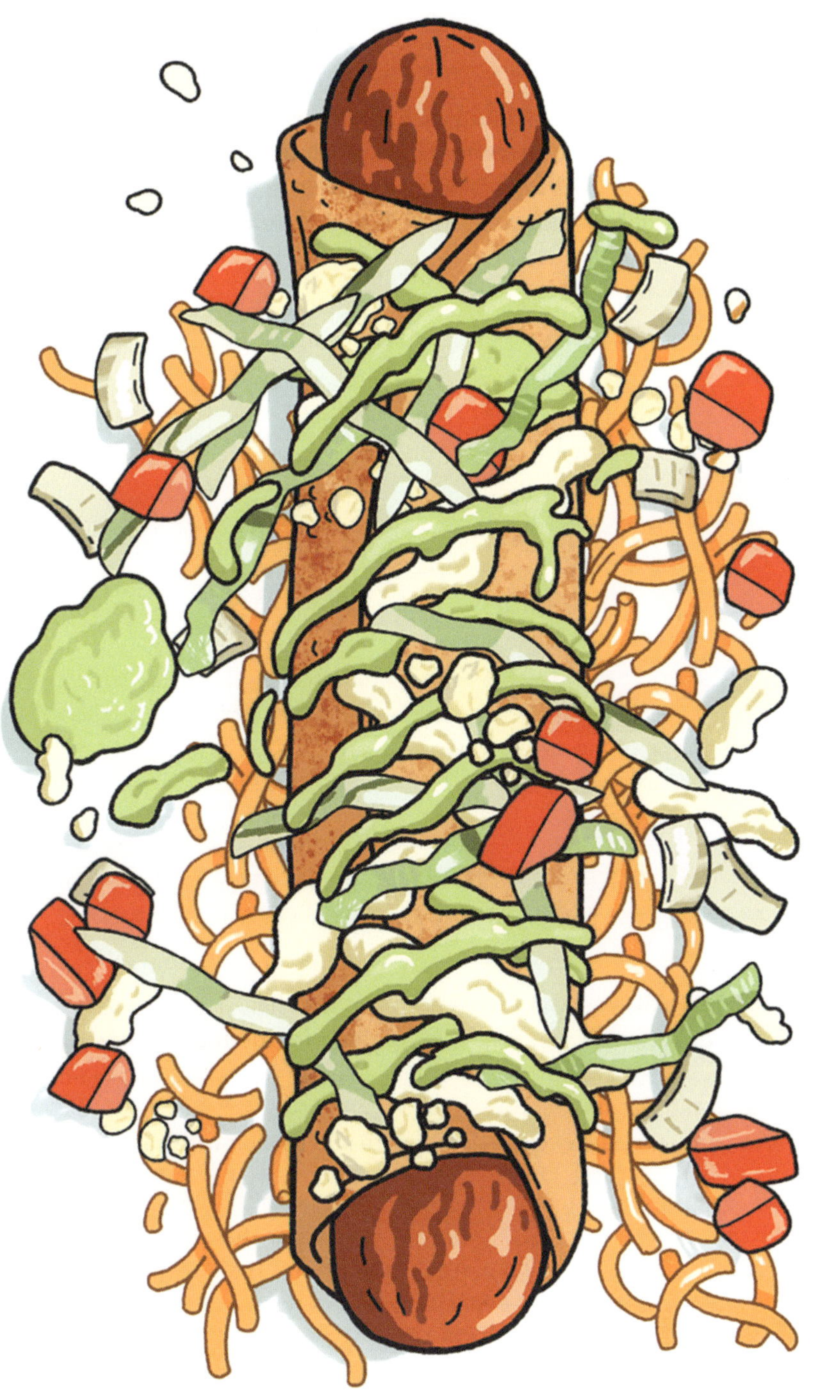

# HOT DOG SPAM MUSUBI

In the years following World War II, the Japanese-inspired Spam musubi became a classic snack or lunch in Hawaii. Similar to onigiri, it consists of sliced and glazed Spam on top of sushi rice and wrapped in nori. With the addition of a trusty hot dog, it's the best sweet-and-salty pairing I've seen since the Baltimore bologna dog (page 46).

**MAKES 8**

1 cup (220 grams) sushi rice

¼ cup (60 grams) granulated sugar

¼ cup (60 ml) soy sauce

2 tablespoons mirin

2 tablespoons vegetable oil, plus more as needed

4 hot dogs, halved

1 can (12 ounces/340 grams) Spam, cut into 8 slices

3 sheets nori, cut into thirds

**1.** Cook the rice according to package instructions. Fluff the rice and keep warm.

**2.** In a small bowl, stir together the sugar, soy sauce, and mirin. Set aside until ready to use.

**3.** Heat the oil in a large skillet over medium heat. Add the hot dogs and cook, turning as needed, until golden, about 3 minutes. Transfer to a cutting board and halve them crosswise. Keep warm.

**4.** Add the Spam to the same skillet (no need to rinse). Cook, turning once, until golden, 6 to 8 minutes. Add the soy sauce mixture to the skillet and bring to a boil, stirring, about 1 minute. Cook until the sauce has reduced to a glaze, about 1 minute more. Remove the pan from the heat and set aside until ready to use.

**5.** Working with one piece of nori at a time, gently toast over a gas flame, waving them so they don't catch fire, about 30 seconds per sheet. If you don't have a gas stove, heat a dry, nonstick skillet over medium-low and cook, flipping once, until lightly toasted, about 10 seconds per side.

**6.** Cut the sheets of nori into 2-inch-wide strips and set aside until ready to use.

**7.** With wet hands, form ¼ cup of the sushi rice into a ball, then press it into the shape of the Spam slice (you can use the Spam can as your guide). Use the bottom of the Spam can to flatten the rice shape, then top it with a hot dog half, followed by a Spam slice.

**8.** Place the rice cake on the piece of nori so that the rice cake is perpendicular to the nori. Using wet fingers, wrap a piece of nori up and around the Spam, sealing the ends of the nori together. Repeat with the remaining ingredients, transfer to plate, and serve.

# HOT DOG CHEESESTEAKS

A Philly cheesesteak in its simplest form consists of cooked sliced rib-eye or top round with melted cheese on a hoagie roll. Here we'll add onions, bell peppers, vinegary hot cherry peppers, a good slather of mayo, and, yes, hot dogs. For a real cheese-steak texture, it's best to slice up your dogs, get them a bit crisp around the edges, and mix them with the onions and peppers.

**MAKES 8**

2 tablespoons vegetable oil

8 hot dogs, thinly sliced on an angle

2 medium green bell peppers, stemmed, seeded, and thinly sliced

2 medium yellow onions, thinly sliced

½ cup (120 grams) seeded and roughly chopped hot cherry peppers

8 slices provolone or white American cheese

4 seeded hoagie rolls (although 8 regular hot dog buns will work fine, too!)

Mayonnaise

***Cheese Tip*** • Feel free to do yours with some bright yellow Cheez Whiz, but sliced provolone or white American is more flavorful and melts beautifully.

**1.** Heat the oil in a large skillet over medium-high heat. Add the hot dogs and cook, stirring, until golden, 3 to 4 minutes, then stir in the bell peppers and onions. Cook, stirring occasionally, until the vegetables are golden and soft, about 8 minutes. Add the cherry peppers and cook until heated through, about 1 minute longer. Shingle the slices of cheese over the top and lower the heat to medium-low. Cook, undisturbed, until the cheese has melted, about 1 minute. Keep warm over low heat.

*(continues)*

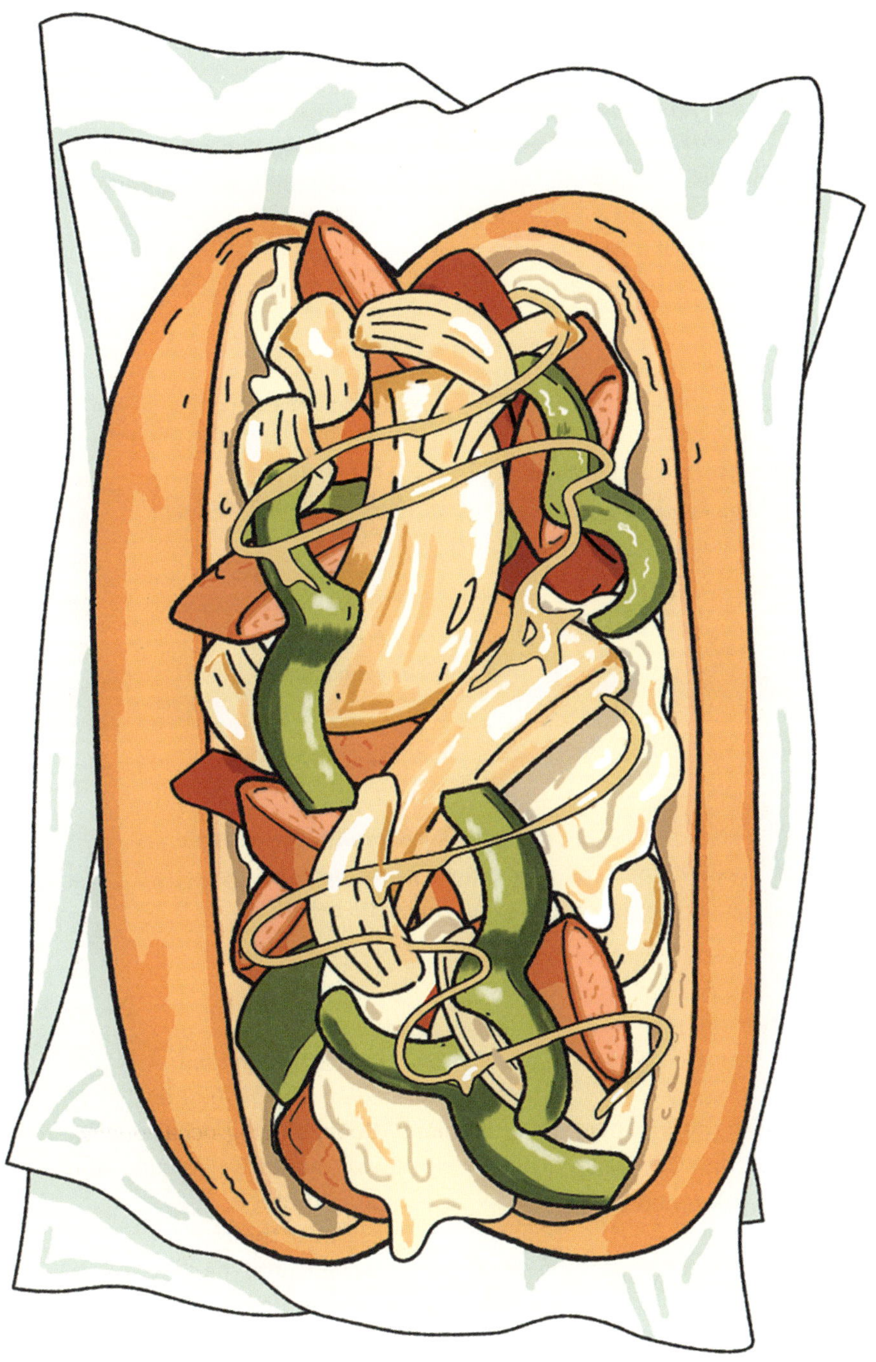

**2.** Meanwhile, spread the inside of the rolls with mayonnaise and, working in batches, toast the insides of the buns in a large skillet over medium heat until golden, about 1½ minutes.

**3.** To assemble, smear the inside of each toasted roll with more mayonnaise, then top with some of the cheesy hot dog and pepper mixture. Slice each roll in half crosswise (if you're using hot dog buns, leave them whole, obviously).

## A Hot Dog Pilgrimage Bucket List

1. Eat back-to-back Coney dogs at Lafayette and American in Detroit.
2. Try a ripper at Rutt's Hut in Clifton, NJ.
3. Stand in line at Pink's Hot Dogs at 2 a.m. in Los Angeles.
4. Order the Recession Special at Gray's Papaya in NYC.
5. Have a Sonoran dog in Tucson, AZ.
6. Hit all nine spots on the Huntington Hot Dog Trail in West Virginia.
7. Eat a lamb dog at Bæjarins Beztu Pylsur in Reykjavík, Iceland.
8. Get a Japadog in Vancouver, Canada.
9. Try a Cachorro Quente in Brazil.
10. Get a hot dog at every baseball stadium—I dare ya.
11. Enter a hot dog eating competition.

# HOT DOG PARMESAN

Give your hot dog the Italian American treatment. The crisp coating, rich tomato sauce, and gooey cheese make this a sandwich that even Tony Soprano would order.

**MAKES 8**

1 cup (190 grams) Italian breadcrumbs

¼ cup (22 grams) grated Parmesan cheese

½ cup (70 grams) all-purpose flour

2 large eggs, lightly beaten

8 hot dogs, butterflied (see page 9)

1 cup (250 ml) vegetable oil

3 cups (750 ml) of your favorite store-bought red sauce

1 pound (454 grams) shredded mozzarella cheese

1 ciabatta loaf, cut crosswise into 8 pieces, 2 inches thick

6 tablespoons (90 ml) olive oil

1 bunch fresh basil

**1.** In a shallow bowl, stir together the breadcrumbs and Parmesan. Place the flour and eggs in two separate shallow bowls. Working with one hot dog at a time, dredge it in the flour, then the egg, and finally the breadcrumb mixture. Place on a large plate. Repeat with the remaining hot dogs.

**2.** Heat the vegetable oil in a large skillet over medium-high heat. Working in batches, add the hot dogs to the skillet, turning once, until golden, about 3 minutes per batch. Add more oil as needed.

**3.** Heat the broiler. Place 1 cup (250 ml) of the red sauce in a large baking dish. Add the hot dogs and top with more red sauce and some mozzarella. Broil the hot dogs until the cheese is golden and bubbling, 3 to 4 minutes.

**4.** Brush the outsides of the bread with the olive oil. Place it cut side up on a sheet pan and broil, turning once, until golden on both sides, about 3 minutes.

**5.** To assemble, place each hot dog in a ciabatta "bun," garnish with some basil, and serve.

# BANH MI HOT DOGS

This classic French-influenced Vietnamese sandwich offers a variety of meat options, as well as pickled vegetables and herbs, all tucked into a soft baguette. The addition of hot dogs here works well; it feels at home among friends. Veggies and fresh herbs help balance the saltiness of the hot dog, and mayonnaise adds creaminess and subtle richness (feel free to use butter or avocado for the same result).

**MAKES 8**

### For the carrot and daikon pickle

1 cup (250 ml) white vinegar

6 tablespoons (90 grams) granulated sugar

8 ounces (225 grams) peeled and julienned carrot

8 ounces (225 grams) peeled and julienned daikon

### For the hot dogs

2 French baguettes, sliced crosswise into 4 pieces each

8 hot dogs, butterflied (see page 9)

Mayonnaise to taste

2 (8 ounce/227 gram) pieces country pâté, thinly sliced

4 to 6 Persian cucumbers, thinly sliced

4 jalapeños, seeded and thinly sliced

1 small bunch cilantro

1 small bunch mint

**1. Make the carrot and daikon pickle:** In a small saucepan, combine the vinegar and sugar. Cook, stirring occasionally, until the sugar is dissolved. Cool slightly. Place the carrot and daikon in a medium bowl and pour the vinegar mixture over the vegetables. Refrigerate until ready to use.

**2. Make the hot dogs:** Heat the oven to 325°F. Bake the bread to warm through, about 5 minutes. Slice each piece of baguette lengthwise and remove some of the inside to make room for the filling.

**3.** Grill the butterflied hot dogs (see page 5).

**4.** To assemble, brush the insides of the bread with the mayonnaise, then add a couple of pieces of the country pâté and a hot dog to the bottom half of each piece of baguette. Top with some pickled carrot and daikon, then a few slices of the cucumbers and jalapeños. Finish with some sprigs of cilantro and mint and serve.

# BREAKFAST SANDWICH DOGS

Any breakfast sandwich worth consuming typically contains eggs, cheese, and some kind of smoked or processed meat—sounds like a job for a hot dog! I love to combine everything on an English muffin, but you could use just about any bun or bread you like.

**MAKES 8**

- ¼ cup (60 grams) ketchup
- ¼ cup (60 grams) sriracha
- Kosher salt and freshly ground black pepper to taste
- 2 tablespoons vegetable oil
- 8 hot dogs, butterflied (see page 9)
- 8 large eggs
- 4 tablespoons (57 grams) unsalted butter
- 8 slices Cheddar cheese
- 8 English muffins, split and toasted

**1.** In a small bowl, stir together the ketchup and sriracha and season with salt and pepper. Set aside until ready to use.

**2.** Heat the oil in a large nonstick skillet over medium heat. Working in batches, add the hot dogs and cook, turning once, until golden, 2 to 3 minutes. Transfer to a cutting board and cut the hot dogs in half, crosswise. Repeat with remaining hot dogs. Keep warm.

**3.** Working in batches, whisk one of the eggs in a small bowl and season with salt and pepper. Melt ½ tablespoon of the butter in a small nonstick skillet over medium heat. Add the egg and cook, tilting the pan to make sure the egg coats it evenly, until the egg is almost set, about 2 minutes. Top with a slice of the cheese and fold the egg in half and cook 30 more seconds, then flip and cook another 30 seconds. Fold it in half again and place on the bottom half of one of the English muffins. Repeat with the remaining eggs and cheese.

**4.** To assemble, place two halves of each hot dog on top of the eggs. Top each with the other half of English muffin and serve with the sriracha-ketchup mixture.

# SCRAMBLED HOT DOGS

This heaping plate of chopped hot dogs and toppings, all piled high on a bun and eaten with a knife and fork, was first served at the Dinglewood Pharmacy in Columbus, Georgia. Cheese, ketchup, and coleslaw are optional additions here, but red hot dogs, pickles, oyster crackers, and a bun drowned in hot dog chili sauce are all necessary. Use either your favorite chili or add your favorite canned hot dog chili sauce.

**SERVES 2**

- 1 can (15 ounces/425 grams) hot dog chili sauce (or use your favorite recipe from the book)
- 1 can (8 ounces/227 grams) tomato sauce
- 2 red hot dogs
- 2 hot dog buns
- 4 slices American cheese, torn into pieces (optional)
- 16 bread-and-butter pickle slices
- Coleslaw (optional)
- Diced yellow onion (optional)
- ½ cup (30 grams) oyster crackers
- Ketchup (optional)
- Yellow mustard (optional)

**1.** In a small saucepan, heat the chili sauce and tomato sauce over medium heat until warmed through, about 10 minutes. Keep warm.

**2.** Boil the hot dogs (see page 5).

**3.** To assemble, open the buns flat and place them onto two different plates, then ladle some of the chili sauce over each. Cut the hot dogs into ½-inch pieces and add them to the buns, then top with some pieces of the cheese, if using, and the pickles. Add coleslaw and onions, then finish with the oyster crackers. Drizzle on ketchup and mustard, if you like, and serve.

# BUFFALO "WING" HOT DOGS

Which is your go-to at the gameday cookout: dogs or wings? We split the difference in this recipe by swapping chicken for hot dogs, and the results are the same: salty, spicy, and perfect. Dip it in a combination of ranch dressing and blue cheese (feel free to throw these into a toasted bun, if you'd like), and don't forget to serve some celery and carrot sticks on the side.

**MAKES 8**

**For the blue cheese ranch dressing**

½ cup (120 grams) mayonnaise

¼ cup (60 grams) sour cream

2 ounces (56 grams) crumbled blue cheese

1 tablespoon minced fresh chives

1 teaspoon garlic powder

1 teaspoon minced fresh dill

¾ teaspoon white vinegar

Kosher salt and freshly ground black pepper to taste

**For the hot dogs**

¼ cup (60 ml) hot sauce, preferably Frank's RedHot

4 tablespoons (56 grams) unsalted butter

½ teaspoon garlic salt

8 hot dogs, sliced on the diagonal into 1-inch-thick pieces

Vegetable oil for deep frying

Celery sticks

Carrot sticks

Celery leaves for garnish

**1. Make the dressing:** In a small bowl, whisk together the mayonnaise and sour cream. Stir in the cheese, chives, garlic powder, dill, and vinegar. Season with salt and pepper and set aside until ready to use.

**2. Make the hot dogs:** In a small skillet, heat the hot sauce, butter, and garlic salt until the butter has melted. Keep warm over low heat until ready to use.

**3.** Deep-fry the hot dogs (see page 6). Carefully transfer the hot sauce mixture to a large bowl, then add the hot dogs and toss to combine. Transfer to a large platter. Serve with the dressing and celery and carrot sticks on the side and garnish with celery leaves.

# Resources

## *Hot Dog Brands*

Nathan's Famous: The Coney Island OG since 1916

Sabrett: Known for their street cart snap and natural casing

Oscar Mayer: The household classic of Wienermobile fame

Ball Park Franks: "They plump when you cook 'em" nostalgia

Hebrew National: All-beef and kosher certified

Vienna Beef: Chicago-style royalty

Boar's Head: Premium deli-quality franks

Kayem: Beloved in New England, often seen at Fenway Park

Hummel Bros.: Connecticut favorite with natural casing

Usinger's: Milwaukee's German-style sausage kings

Koegel's: Michigan pride, especially in Flint and Detroit

Schaller & Weber: NYC's old-world German butcher shop

Esposito's: Philly's specialty butcher dogs

Snake River Farms: Wagyu beef hot dogs

Niman Ranch: Ethically raised, high-quality meat franks

Organic Prairie: Organic and family-farm produced

Porter Road: Pasture-raised, artisanal sausages and franks

Applegate Naturals: Natural and uncured options

Wellshire Farms: Known for natural casing and nitrate-free

Saugy's: Based in Rhode Island and snapping since 1869

North Country Smokehouse: Has bits of maple cured bacon

## *Condiments & Toppings*

Mustard: Gulden's (especially their spicy brown!), French's, Maille Dijon, Grey Poupon, Dietz & Watson

Ketchup: Heinz (the only acceptable option, let's be honest here)

Mayo: Hellman's, Duke's, Kewpie

Sauerkraut: Cleveland Kraut, Wildbrine, Bubbies

Pickles: Maille, Vlasic, Clausen, Mt. Olive

Crispy Shallots: Maesri

Celery Salt: McCormick, Spiceology

Spices: Old Bay Seasoning

**Kimchi:** Mother in Law's Kimchi
**Hot Dog Chili Sauce:** Steve & Ed's, Castleberry's, Vietti
**Chili Crisp:** Fly By Jing, Lao Gan Ma
**Bacon:** Smithfield's, Benton's, Oscar Mayer
**Potato Chips:** Deep River, Cape Cod, Wise, Utz, Ruffles

## Buns

**Martin's:** Soft, sweet, buttery, made with potatoes
**Pepperidge Farms:** Sturdy, classic bakery-style
**Arnold:** Hearty, dense crumb

## Hot Dog Stands

There are so many great hot dog stands around the United States, and here are just a handful. Send me your recs!

**Attman's Deli:** Baltimore
**Yeti Dogs:** Anchorage
**Nathan's Famous:** Coney Island
**Pink's Hot Dogs:** Los Angeles
**Ben's Chili Bowl:** Washington, DC
**The Wieners Circle:** Chicago
**Gray's Papaya:** New York City
**Rutt's Hut:** Clifton, NJ
**Nogales Hot Dogs:** Phoenix
**Frostop Drive-In:** Huntington, WV
**American Coney Island** and **Lafayette Coney Island:** Detroit
**Dinglewood Pharmacy:** Columbus, GA
**The Varsity:** Atlanta
**Gene & Jude's:** River Grove, IL
**Costco Food Court:** Nationwide
**Olneyville New York System:** Providence, RI
**Jimmy Buff's:** Newark, NJ
**Dickie Dee's:** Newark, NJ
**Famous Lunch:** Troy, NY

# Index

## Acknowledgments

I'm a lucky girl that gets to work on a cookbook dedicated to hot dogs. I'd like to first and foremost thank water for keeping me hydrated and not nearly as puffy from the sodium intake during my recipe testing journey. Thanks to my parents, Teresa and Manouch, and my sister, Amanda, for listening to me ramble about hot dogs at most family dinners. You guys are always so supportive and loving, and I don't know what I'd do without you.

Getting people to help test recipes for this book was the easiest thing, so thank you to all of my volunteers for your insights and help: Agatha Kulaga, Andrew DiBenedetto, Ashley Berman, Jon Kung, Jane Garofalo, Marie Carbone, Elena Yamamoto, Rachel Mossberg, Eleanor Galloway, Felicia Campbell, Ben Turley, Laura Sant, Kim McNally, Jose Prieto, Lili Dagan, and Edwin Santacruz.

A very special thanks to Judy Haubert and Michelle Warner for each coming over and spending a full day with me in the kitchen; it was nice to have company cooking for a change. Thanks to Jen Kelly and Nick Rose for your hot dog expertise (for Seattle dogs and Montreal Steamies, respectfully).

JJ Goode, my fairy dog-father. You're the best. I owe you a couple dogs. To my agent, Kari Stuart. I don't know what I'd do without you. The three of us need another dinner soon (Applebee's?).

Thanks to the team at Workman for putting together such an incredible book, including designer Reagan Ruff and production editor Kate Karol. My editor, Danny Cooper: Thank you for all your helpful notes and queries and for pushing this book to begin with. Hot dogs really are the best.

Eve Anderson, your illustrations made this book that much more fun and playful. Thank you!

I ate a lot of hot dogs to prepare for this book, not just while writing it, but over the course of my entire life. I'll never not go out of my way to stop somewhere for a hot dog. I know there's a dirty rumor that eating one hot dog can take 36 minutes off your life, and if that's the case, I'd be dead by now. Happily, I might add. TLDR: eat the hot dog(s).

**Farideh Sadeghin** is a food writer and recipe developer based in Brooklyn, New York. She loves anything chocolate, ice-cold martinis, and, of course, hot dogs. Subscribe to her newsletter and YouTube channel for more.

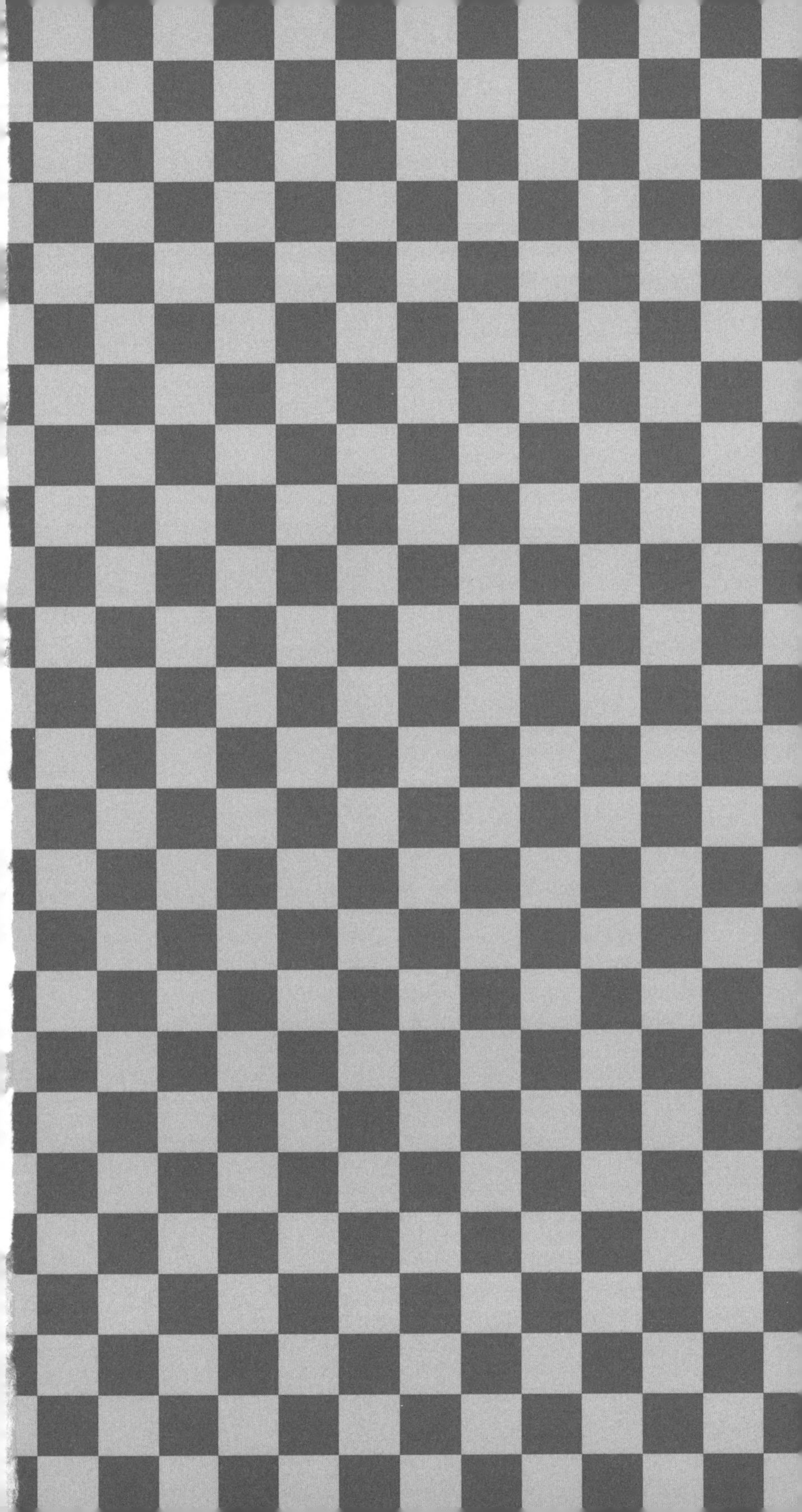

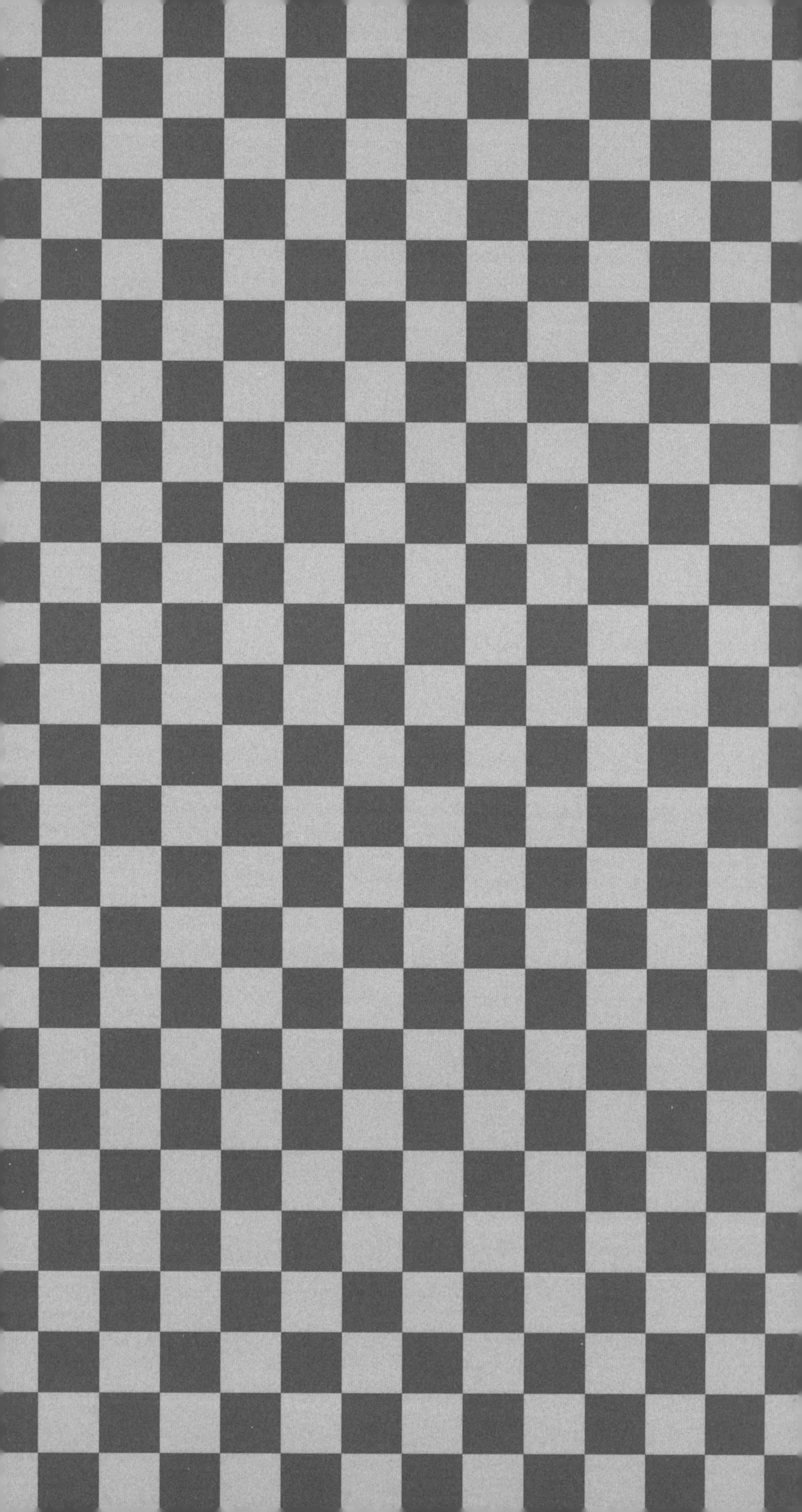